Why The CIA Killed JFK and Malcolm X

The Secret Drug Trade in Laos

Why The CIA Killed JFK and Malcolm X

The Secret Drug Trade in Laos

John Koerner

Winchester, UK
Washington, USA

First published by Chronos Books, 2014
Chronos Books is an imprint of John Hunt Publishing Ltd., Laurel House, Station Approach,
Alresford, Hants, SO24 9JH, UK
office1@jhpbooks.net
www.johnhuntpublishing.com

For distributor details and how to order please visit the 'Ordering' section on our website.

A CIP catalogue record for this book is available from the British Library.

Design: Lee Nash

Printed and bound by CPI Group (UK) Ltd, Croydon, CR0 4YY

We operate a distinctive and ethical publishing philosophy in all
areas of our business, from our global network of authors to
production and worldwide distribution.

CONTENTS

Introduction

This is a dangerous book. If you have any investment in pursuing the truth, then what you will find within will be at times enlightening, and shocking. Mainstream, packaged history that is freshly sliced for America's students in neatly compartmentalized boxes barely gives a whisper of the word "conspiracy," as if it were a disease to avoid exposing to the innocent.

Yet as historians, our goal should always be to pursue the truth, no matter how uncomfortable the answers might be. Facts are stubborn things, as John Adams was fond of saying. History at its best should bend or break our preconceived notions of what a static historical record should consist of. Conspiracies are far more common than we imagine, and one should never have to apologize for proffering them as solutions to historical mysteries. Historians should not have to whisper the word for fear of academic reprisal.

For truly, what are conspiracies? Put simply, it is when a group of people plan to execute a specific task. Humans are social creatures. We work together to accomplish an endless number of ideas throughout the course of our lives. It is counterintuitive to think otherwise. It is time to move conspiracies from the realm of the paranormal to that of the normal.

Ironically though, there is nothing normal about the conspiracy to assassinate President John F. Kennedy. So much has been written about this man's death, now over half a century since that tragic day in Dallas. The astute reader might wonder what more could be added to what has already been exhaustively written. The answer is two-fold.

Much to the credit of many hardworking historians in the past five decades, Kennedy's assassination has been examined from the standpoint of how it happened, and who was responsible. Very little time has been spent trying to examine why he was killed, especially how a little known country in Southeast Asia named Laos hastened his demise.

I will argue in this book that the CIA's secret drug trade in Laos, and the president's effort to end it, provided the primary motive that the CIA needed to assassinate the president. A lot of effort has made to examine the president's Vietnam policy, which does link to this as we will see, but precious little attention has been paid to the opium trade in Laos that was making the CIA wealthy and powerful beyond its wildest dreams. This book will chronicle the president's secret war with the CIA over Laos, a high stakes game that cost him his life.

The second addition to the historical record that this book will contribute is an attempt to link the JFK assassination with the other three major assassinations of the 1960s: Malcolm X, Martin Luther King, and Robert F. Kennedy. Not enough attention has been paid to why these leaders were killed as well. We will see that all four of the assassinations are linked together, all funded and executed by the CIA to silence the four most vocal leaders who were opposed to the agency's pro-war, and pro-drug policy in Laos and Vietnam.

Finally, we will examine the impact this has had on the course of history, and imagine a world where a part of the United States government never saw fit to overturn the will of the American people, and rob the nation of four of the most important leaders in U.S. history for its own power and financial gain.

John Koerner
February, 2014

Chapter One

A Hated President

President John F. Kennedy was skilled at many things throughout the course of his life. He was an award winning author, a war hero, an athlete, and a doting father, with a sense of style and grace rarely seen in the presidency. He also was adept at making a variety of powerful enemies throughout the course of his administration. By the time of his death, anti-Catholics, southern racists, the Mafia, Fidel Castro, the FBI, the CIA, and the military would all have moments of bitter clashes with the commander in chief. The assassination of JFK did not occur in a vacuum. In order to understand why the CIA wanted the president dead, and felt justified in doing so we need to examine the escalating tension within the Kennedy administration. Each section in chapter one will deal with a different source of anger directed at the president. It was within this climate of hate that made the assassination inevitable. Some of this conflict was not even his fault. We can begin with an issue that came up even before he became president: his faith.

The "Papist" Presidency

Being a Roman Catholic throughout much of American history was a dangerous proposition. Many were ostracized for simply being a member of this religion, and were denied access to power and equal rights for centuries. Many Protestants in positions of power felt that Catholics could not serve two masters, that given the chance they would be loyal to the papacy and could not possibly be patriotic Americans, much less trusted in positions of power like in the military or politics. Some even went so far as to believe that the reason all the millions of Italian, Polish, and Irish immigrants were crashing our borders was that many foreign governments wanted these "papists" to undermine our democracy.

The KKK, the YMCA, and the American Party (otherwise known as the Know Nothing Party) were all in part founded on the idea of combating the influence of Catholics in our culture. From 1887 until the 1920s, the American Protective Association promoted violent anti-Catholic rhetoric. Founder Henry F. Bowers spread misinformation that a papal decree absolved all allegiance to the United States. Bowers even went so far as to engage in outright demagoguery by claiming that Catholics were going to massacre all Protestants using a secret stash of weapons being hidden in the cellars of Catholic churches. The date of retribution was allegedly set for September 5, 1893, when the "papists" would unleash their collective fury on the terrified American people.[1] When the day of reckoning arrived nothing happened, but the hatred did not stop.

It is perhaps therefore not surprising that in this oppressive climate, John F. Kennedy remains the only Catholic ever elected to the presidency. It was an issue he had to confront directly during his 1960 campaign for president. Norman Vincent Peale, perhaps the nation's most prominent Protestant minister openly questioned whether Kennedy would bring his foreign policy "into line with Vatican objectives."[2] The Massachusetts senator made a speech in front of the Greater Houston Ministerial Association at the Rice Hotel in Houston, Texas, on September 12, 1960, to respond to these charges. This would be the same hotel he would stay at the night before his assassination in Dallas just over three years later.[3] Earlier that day he was greeted by hostile crowds with signs reading "We Don't Want the Kremlin or the Vatican." JFK would speak forcefully in Houston about his political independence and the separation of church and state.

I believe in an America that is officially neither Catholic, Protestant nor Jewish; where no public official either requests

2

or accepts instructions on public policy from the Pope...or any other ecclesiastical source...For while this year it may be a Catholic against whom the finger of suspicion is pointed, in other years it has been – and may someday be again – a Jew, or a Quaker, or a Unitarian, or a Baptist. It was Virginia's harassment of Baptist preachers, for example, that led to Jefferson's statute of religious freedom. Today, I may be the victim, but tomorrow it may be you...

This is the kind of America I believe in – and this is the kind of America I fought for in the South Pacific, and the kind my brother died for in Europe. No one suggested then that we might have a divided loyalty, that we did not believe in liberty, or that we belonged to a disloyal group that threatened ..."the freedoms for which our forefathers died."...

But let me stress again that these are my views. For contrary to common newspaper usage, I am not the Catholic candidate for President. I am the Democratic Party's candidate for President who happens also to be a Catholic. I do not speak for my church on public matters; and the church does not speak for me.[4]

When the speech was finished the Protestant ministers engaged in a heated question and answer session with Kennedy, attempting to, at various times, trap him into going back on the independent platform he had laid out in his speech.

The most aggressive questioning came from Pastor K.O. White of Houston's First Baptist Church who said, "Your church has stated that it has the privilege and the right and the responsibility to direct its members in various areas of life, including the political realm." White's next sentence summed up over 100 years of Protestant fears. "We believe that history and observation indicate that it has done so. And we raise the question because we would like to know, if you are elected President and your church elects to use that privilege and obligation, what your response will be."[5]

Kennedy calmly stated, as he already had in his speech, "If my church attempted to influence me in any way...then I would reply to them that this was an improper action on their part, that it was one to which I could not subscribe, that I was opposed to it, and that it would be an unfortunate breach of – an interference, with the American political system."[6]

Despite the candidate's best efforts, many Americans still refused to vote for him simply because he was Catholic, perhaps at least in part accounting for the slim margin of victory in the 1960 popular vote total: JFK 49.7% to Richard Nixon's 49.5%.[7]

After the president's assassination, a number of Protestant ministers in Dallas expressed some remorse that this climate of hate may have contributed to the president's death. The Rev. Charles Denman of the Wesley Methodist Church said, "In Dallas entire sermons have been devoted to damning the Kennedy administration... and they have been delivered from Methodist pulpits," said Denman. "In the name of the church, men and women have sown seeds of discord, distrust and hate and have called it witnessing for Christ. As a church we are sick. God have mercy on us."[8]

The Rev. William Holmes of the Northhaven Methodist Church said, "There is no city in the United States which in recent months and years has been more acquiescent toward its extremists than Dallas, Texas. We... have gone quietly about our work and leisure, forfeiting the city's image to the hate mongers and reactionaries in our midst. The spirit of assassination has been with us for some time."[9]

"The spirit of assassination" was indeed alive and well in Dallas, but not just because of the president's religion. The south was also violently opposed to Kennedy's embracement of the Civil Rights Movement.

JFK vs. the South

When the news of President Kennedy's death was announced to the nation, the grief was too much for many of America's school children to handle. Millions of students began to sob uncontrollably. CBS News anchor Walter Cronkite said that "the nation is in almost uncontrollable shock. Schools have to be dismissed. My own school was dismissed because the children were weeping so much they could not concentrate."[10]

That certainly was not the case in a Columbus, Mississippi, elementary school where students responded with spontaneous applause when the news of JFK's death was announced over the loud speakers.[11] More southern hatred came from Ted Dealey, owner of the *Dallas Morning News*. He told Kennedy at a White House luncheon in October 1961 that what the country needed was "a man on horseback to lead this nation and many people in Texas and the Southwest think that you are riding Caroline's tricycle."[12] Dealey also approved a hate-laced full page advertisement attacking the president that appeared in his newspaper on the morning of the assassination. The ad was paid for by the Hunt family, an oil-rich Texas clan based in Dallas.[13] Ted Dealey had assumed command of the *Dallas Morning News* after the death of his father, George Bannerman Dealey, whom Dealey Plaza is named after, of course the site of President Kennedy's assassination.[14]

As JFK began his trip to Texas he remarked to an aide that he was "heading into nut country."[15] One of the president's most bitter enemies was in Dallas during the week of the assassination too, spewing hate. Alabama Governor George Wallace, a blatant racist and vocal defender of segregation, said "We resent Washington telling us how to run our schools. Why, they've had to build extra bridges across the Potomac just for the people leaving Washington since they integrated the schools there," an obvious, blatant lie. Wallace, who arrived on a plane with Confederate flag markings, said that "we Alabama people ought to be telling (Washington) how to run their schools."[16]

The intense southern hatred directed toward John F. Kennedy was largely due to his progressive record on Civil Rights. Up until the 1960s, presidents cared precious little about the African American race choosing to ignore Amendments to the Constitution that guaranteed equal rights and suffrage for all people. The southern courts were a disgrace, littered with rigged juries. The South had descended into blatant, oppressive segregation for a century; a virtual Confederate States of the Ku Klux Klan.

Kennedy's efforts to end this began even before he became president. During the 1960 campaign, a month before the election, Senator Kennedy, and his brother Robert, arranged for the release of Martin Luther King from a Georgia prison, where many felt King's four month sentence would lead to his lynching.[17]

JFK's efforts to help African Americans continued during his presidency. In his first year as commander in chief he instructed the Interstate Commerce Commission to end discrimination in interstate public transportation.[18] On November 20, 1962, the president signed Executive Order 11063 which mandated an end to discrimination in housing. The stroke of the president's pen "prohibited federally funded housing agencies from denying housing or funding for housing to anyone based on their race, color, creed or national origin."[19]

JFK also appointed over fifty African American men and women to key positions of power in his administration. These included:

- **Andrew T. Hatcher,** associate White House press secretary, the first black man to hold that post. 200 times he filled in for Press Secretary Pierre Salinger
- **Dr. Robert Weaver,** director of the Housing and Home Finance Agency, "the highest appointive federal office ever held by an American Negro," the *Chicago Defender* said

when Weaver received the NAACP's Spingarn Medal on June 5, 1962

- **George L. P. Weaver,** assistant secretary of labor for Internal Affairs
- **Carl Rowan,** deputy assistant secretary of state for Public Affairs
- **Dr. Grace Hewell,** program coordination officer, Dept. of Health, Education and Welfare
- **Lt. Commander Samuel Gravely,** of the *U.S.S. Falgout*, the first black Navy commander to lead a combat ship
- **John P. Duncan,** commissioner of the District of Columbia
- **Clifford Alexander, Jr.,** national security council member
- **A. Leon Higginbotham,** a member of the Federal Trade Commission, the first African American to be appointed to a federal regulatory agency
- **Ambassadors:** Carl Rowan, to Finland; Clifton Wharton, to Norway; and Mercer Cook, to Niger
- **U.S. attorneys:** Cecil Poole, Northern California; and Merle McCurdy, Northern Ohio
- **Federal judges:** James Benton Parsons, Northern District of Illinois, the first black federal district court judge; Wade McCree, Eastern District of Michigan; Marjorie Lawson, Juvenile Court of the District of Columbia; and, Thurgood Marshall, the Second Circuit, U.S. Court of Appeals[20]

Another African American "first" for the JFK administration was when President Kennedy appointed Abraham Bolden to be the first African American Secret Service agent. In 1961, Bolden began his service to the agency, but was quickly reassigned to Chicago after complaining about unfair treatment by his fellow agents. While in that city he helped uncover a plot to assassinate President Kennedy that was supposed to take place on November 2, 1963. The Secret Service arrested two suspects, but let them go. They also never forwarded this information to the

Warren Commission that was appointed by President Lyndon Johnson in 1964 to investigate the JFK assassination. Bolden was not assigned to protect the president in Dallas, and later went on to criticize the drunken behavior of the agents which he felt helped contribute to the president's death.[21]

This was the first time in American history that a president had appointed this many African Americans, and not just to figure-head positions, but to important positions of influence. The appointments that Kennedy made to his team were certainly historic, yet integrating the southern school systems was the most deadly of the president's civil rights strategies. JFK used military and political pressure to end segregation at the University of Mississippi in 1962, resulting in two deaths and dozens of injuries due to clashes between the U.S. military and local racist mobs.[22] The University of Alabama was integrated in 1963 as well, despite the personal protests of Governor George Wallace.

"If an American, because his skin is dark, cannot eat lunch in a restaurant open to the public, if he cannot send his children to the best school available," Kennedy said in 1963, "if he cannot vote for the public officials who represent him, if, in short, he cannot enjoy the full and free life which all of us want, then who among us would be content to have the color of his skin changed and stand in his place? Who among us would then be content with the counsels of patience and delay?"[23]

Yet the most controversial of all was the president's speech to the nation on June 11, 1963, when he proposed the largest Civil Rights Bill in American history that would end discrimination of any kind for all people in the United States. "One hundred years have passed since President Lincoln freed the slaves, yet their heirs, their grandsons, are not fully free," Kennedy said. "They are not yet freed from the bonds of injustice. They are not yet freed from social and economic oppression. And this nation, for all its hopes and all its boasts, will not be fully free until all its citizens are free."[24]

Bumper stickers soon started to spring up in the south saying, "KO the Kennedys."[25] In less than six months the president would be dead.

"A Thousand Pieces"

In the early 1960s an unholy alliance was forming between the Mafia, the CIA, and what President Dwight Eisenhower would call the "military industrial complex." Kennedy would end up butting heads with all three of these groups during his short time in office.

The CIA was on a bit of a winning streak when it reached 1960. In recent years they had successfully installed American puppet governments in Greece, Turkey, Iran, and Guatemala, often overturning the will of the people, and instilling violent anti-American sentiment in the process. But 1960 marked a turning point. The Eisenhower administration and the CIA enlisted the help of the American Mafia to aid in its removal of three foreign leaders. They were Rafael Trujillo of the Dominican Republic, Patrice Lumumba of the Congo, and Fidel Castro of Cuba.[26] The first two were executed with ruthless efficiency, but the third assignment was a bit more problematic.

The plan to remove Castro lingered on into the Kennedy administration. This of course was an operation hatched under Eisenhower. The CIA was feeling perhaps a bit too overconfident that whatever mission it undertook, they would achieve success. Failure would not be an option. Failure would be devastating to their image and the collective hubris of an agency that expected full cooperation from the presidents. Presidents Harry Truman and Dwight Eisenhower rarely told the CIA no for its exotic clandestine operations. Cuba would be just another feather in their cap. Castro would be removed, and the perceived threat of a Communist government off the coast of Florida would cease to exist.

However, the plan went horribly wrong. The 1,400 anti-

Castro Cubans that the CIA trained were no match for Castro's army who quickly captured, tortured, and killed them. By April 19, 1961, the so-called "Bay of Pigs Invasion" was over. The fallout would be enormous. During the invasion, the CIA advised JFK that he should start bombing Cuba, or approve an invasion of the island by the U.S. military. The president quickly rejected these ideas; not wanting to attack a nation without provocation which he felt might provoke a wider war with the Soviet Union. The communists might retaliate by seeking to bomb American-held installations in Europe like West Berlin, for example.[27]

Privately, the commander in chief speculated that the CIA may have been trying to manipulate him into starting a war with the Soviet Union by deliberately causing this invasion to fail, thereby forcing him to bomb Cuba to save the doomed invaders. He was not going to fall into that trap. Kennedy eventually fired CIA Director Allen Dulles in September 1961, and Deputy Director for Plans Richard Bissell, who left office in February 1962.[28] On January 31, 1962, General Charles P. Cabell, deputy director of the CIA, was forced to resign as well. His brother Earle Cabell was the mayor of Dallas during the assassination of President Kennedy.[29] Dulles, Bissell, and Cabell were all holdovers from the Eisenhower Administration. Kennedy angrily told an adminis-tration official, that he vowed to "splinter the CIA in a thousand pieces and scatter it to the winds."[30]

As part of this effort just a few months later on June 28, 1961, the president issued National Security Action Memorandums 55, 56, and 57. These were orders by the commander in chief to restructure nearly the entire military industrial complex. The president ordered that covert paramilitary operations of the CIA be shifted to the Defense Department and the Joint Chiefs of Staff. In NSAM 55, JFK states that:

a. I regard the Joint Chiefs of Staff as my principal military advisor responsible both for initiating advice to me and for responding to requests for advice. I expect their advice to come to me direct and unfiltered.

b. The Joint Chiefs of Staff have a responsibility for the defense of the nation in the Cold War similar to that which they have in conventional hostilities. They should know the military and paramilitary forces and resources available to the Department of Defense, verify their readiness, report on their accuracy, and make appropriate recommendations for their expansion and improvement. I look to the Chiefs to contribute dynamic and imaginative leadership in contributing to the success of the military and paramilitary aspects of Cold War programs.[31]

The key sentence was that the Chiefs would now be the "principal military advisor," in other words, not the CIA. The advice must be "direct and unfiltered," implying that in the past the CIA had lied to him, and hid information from him. The president was also saying that he was now counting on the Chiefs' leadership in "paramilitary" operations, an area that had been assigned to the CIA. This World War Two veteran was seeking to reestablish the model of "conventional" warfare that worked during World War Two when there was no CIA, and the president and the Chiefs operated in tandem. NSAM 55 was a severe blow to the power, influence, and role of the Central Intelligence Agency. So was NSAM 57, issued that same day. It read in part:

Any proposed paramilitary operation in the concept state will be presented to the Strategic Resources Group for initial consideration and for approval as necessary by the President. Thereafter, the SRG will assign primary responsibility for planning, for interdepartmental coordination and for execution to the task force, department or individual best qualified to carry forward the operation to success, and will indicate supporting responsibilities. Under this principle, the Department of Defense will normally receive responsibility for overt paramilitary operations. Where such an operation is to be wholly covert or disavowable, it may be assigned to CIA, provided that it is within the normal capabilities of the agency. Any large paramilitary operation wholly or partly covert which requires significant numbers of military trained personnel, amounts to military equipment which exceed normal CIA-controlled stocks and/or military experience of a kind and level peculiar to the Armed services is properly the primary responsibility of the Department of Defense with the CIA in a supporting role.[32]

This directive from the president meant that now the CIA was going to have to move through several oversight bodies before its operations could get approved, including the Strategic Resources Group, the Department of Defense, and of course the president himself. Also, large paramilitary operations would now be handled by the Department of Defense, and the CIA would now only have a "supporting role" in such operations.

These documents collectively shifted power in the military industrial complex away from the CIA and placed most of it back in the hands of the president, the Defense Department, and the Joint Chiefs of Staff. The president was ordering the military to take power away from the CIA and handle most of the paramilitary operations within the Department of Defense. This was a bold move. The president did not trust the CIA. At that point, as we will see in chapter three, they were attempting to manipulate him into going to war in Vietnam, Laos, and Cuba, all of which he eventually rejected. The Joint Chiefs were not supportive of JFK's policies of peace either. They pushed for invasions in Laos, Vietnam, and Cuba just as much as the CIA did. But these directives made it clear that even though the Chiefs and the Defense

Department would have more paramilitary responsibility, they will still answer to him. Not only that, this was a bold political move, essentially pitting these two entities (CIA and Chiefs) against each other in a struggle for military power. Perhaps the CIA would begin to resent the Chiefs for taking their power, and thus become more isolated. The Chiefs might now become more pro-Kennedy with a reassertion of their power, handed to them by the president. Another factor in this equation was that JFK knew that if power shifted to the Joint Chiefs of Staff, they would be required to answer to Secretary of Defense Robert McNamara, a loyal Kennedy cabinet member who was not a war hawk and could be trusted by JFK.

55, 56, and 57 add up to 168 pieces scattered to the winds.

The situation with the CIA grew even more volatile with JFK after the Cuban Missile Crisis. There is no need to rehash the entire history of those thirteen days in October 1962 when the Soviet Union put nuclear missiles in Cuba, and brought the world to the brink of mutual assured destruction. However, many in the CIA felt that the president's peaceful solution to the crisis was unacceptable. JFK made a deal with Russian Premier Nikita Khrushchev to never invade Cuba in exchange for a Russian withdrawal of the missiles. The military and the CIA felt that the president had caved in and was soft on Communism.

After the Cuban Missile Crisis, a number of additional steps were taken by JFK in an attempt to end the Cold War and promote peace. The president opened a direct communication "hotline" that linked Washington to Moscow to foster greater understanding and dialogue between the two superpowers. This was established on June 20, 1963.[33] Kennedy also called for an end to the so-called "space race", by planning a joint Russian-American moon landing by the end of the 1960s, and the Soviets were prepared to accept this offer.[34] Less than four months before his assassination, Kennedy signed a nuclear test ban treaty with the USSR on August 5, 1963, saying that "if we cannot end our differences, at least we can help make the world a safe place for diversity." [35]

And perhaps most importantly the commander in chief put forth a plan to end the Vietnam War by 1965. The Sec Def Conference of May 1963, and another meeting of key JFK advisors in Hawaii in November 1963, both reiterated and recommended a phased "Vietnamization" withdrawal from Vietnam within two years.[36] The president signed National Security Action Memorandum 263 on October 11, 1963, to bring home the first 1,000 advisors of the meager total of 16,000, by December 1963.[37]

As we will see in chapter four, all of these efforts to promote peace undermined the CIA's efforts to stay in Southeast Asia to make a profit on the opium trade. War was too profitable to just sit idly by and let the president threaten the existence of this agency. The CIA engaged in a number of actions to retaliate, including an attempt to destroy the Peace Corps. This of course was JFK's pride and joy; established by executive order on March 1, 1961, to promote peace, end poverty, and push the idea of civic service to your country.[38] To plan to turn an agency designed to promote peace, into an agency designed to promote war, as the CIA intended, verges on the diabolical.

President Kennedy had a conversation with Peace Corps Director Sargent Shriver on April 2, 1963, about this issue. Shriver called the president because he suspected a group of new recruits "looked suspicious" and were probably undercover CIA agents. The Corps had already rejected dozens of applicants who worked for the CIA.[39] The president responded that he was "very anxious about this" and such an infiltration could ruin and "discredit" the whole purpose of the Corps.[40] Kennedy speechwriter Theodore Sorenson has written extensively how the Peace Corps had to work exhaustively to keep the Corps free of agents, especially in its early years.[41] Corps organizers even had to worry about CIA operatives approaching corps members to enlist them as undercover agents who could secretly infiltrate the agency. New recruits were advised to report any contact to their supervisors.[42]

Because of this history of trying to turn the Peace Corps into a CIA front to promote war, there is still an inherent lack of trust within the Corps towards that agency. "If you have ever worked for the CIA, you are permanently ineligible for employment at the Peace Corps. Do not submit an application for employment with the Peace Corps," reads the "Eligibility" section on the Peace Corps website. "If you currently live with someone who works for the CIA, you will not be eligible for employment with the Peace Corps until you have ceased living with that person for at least six months. Do not submit an application for employment with the Peace Corps until that waiting period has elapsed."[43]

The second of many other forms of countermeasures that the CIA did to work against the president's efforts toward peace was to set in motion a new plan to get rid of Fidel Castro, and provoke a war with the Soviet Union. The plan, called Operation Northwoods, called for staging fake acts of domestic terrorism, all of which would kill Americans, but would wrongly be blamed on Fidel Castro. This was the brainchild of CIA agent Edward Landsdale who had been with the agency since its inception. He presented this idea to the Joint Chiefs of Staff that the CIA would of course carry out this mission, violating its oath to refrain from domestic operations. In theory, once the attacks were staged, the public would demand war with Cuba, which would violate the agreement JFK made with the Soviets to end the Cuban Missile Crisis. This would begin World War Three. Many in the CIA and the military felt JFK gave in too easily to the Russians during that crisis and still wanted Castro gone. The public did not feel the same way. Most lauded the president's handling of the crisis. Bombing or invading Cuba, as the military pushed the commander in chief to do, would surely have provoked a counterattack and nuclear war. Defense Secretary

Robert McNamara shut down Operation Northwoods in March 1963.[44]

Perhaps the CIA was getting too powerful, expanding upon and violating its intended purpose. The agency's founding father, President Harry Truman, certainly thought so. Exactly one month after the assassination, the former president wrote a revealing column that appeared in the *Washington Post*.

"For some time I have been disturbed by the way the CIA has been diverted from its original assignment," wrote Truman. "It has become an operational and at times a policy-making arm of the government. This has led to trouble and may have compounded our difficulties in several explosive areas." He further stated that the CIA's "operational duties" should be "terminated" and that his original directors were men of "the highest character, patriotism, and integrity," implying, of course, that recent ones were not. One of those recent ones, Allen Dulles, tried to get Truman to retract this article but he would not. In fact, Truman went even further in his criticism the following year by telling *Look Magazine* that he never intended the CIA to get involved in "strange activities."[45]

One of those "strange activities" of course was to plan and execute the assassination of the nation's 35th president. It was becoming increasingly clear to those in the CIA that JFK was going to get a second term. His handling of the Cuban Missile Crisis, and continued efforts at peace, were giving him high approval ratings. In March 1963, he enjoyed a 70% approval rating, and the following month nearly three-fourths of the nation said they expected him to be reelected. A mock up poll of JFK against Republican Barry Goldwater (who in 1964 would get the GOP nomination) had Kennedy trouncing him 67% to 27%.[46]

Four more years could not be tolerated.

Chapter Two

A Public Execution

Before we can make the case that the CIA was coordinating a secret and lucrative drug trade in Laos, and that JFK was essentially the only thing in their way from allowing this to flourish, we need to briefly present the evidence that this agency was in fact directly responsible for his murder. Once we establish their guilt we can move on to the drug trafficking motive, a connection that no historian has yet made to JFK's assassination, much less to the subsequent ones that the agency planned and executed.

To be clear, the purpose of this book is not to prove *that* the CIA killed President John F. Kennedy. The purpose is to explain *why*; to argue that JFK's effort to end the CIA's opium trade in Laos provided the primary motivation to plan and execute his assassination. Given that fact, it would be irresponsible and a huge oversight to fail to establish their complicity before we can break that new ground. In other words, if this were a court case, no jury would convict a suspect purely based on motive. There also needs to be proof that the suspect committed the crime. Therefore, in chapter two we will briefly examine the facts that have convinced many historians that this agency was in fact directly responsible for Kennedy's assassination, and then move on. Chapter three will serve as a closing argument, to provide the jury with a powerful new motive to hand back the only logical verdict: guilty.

Proving the Conspiracy

Let us start with the crime scene. The facts are all ingrained in the memories of those who lived through those tragic days. On November 22, 1963, President John F. Kennedy was visiting Dallas on a campaign swing with his wife Jackie, riding of course in an open car through downtown Dallas, with Texas Governor John Connally seated in front of him with his wife, Nellie. Around 12:30 p.m. several shots rang out as the motorcade passed through Dealey Plaza, wounding the president and the governor. JFK was rushed to Parkland Memorial Hospital where he died just after 1 p.m.

President Lyndon Johnson appointed Chief Justice Earl Warren to head a commission to investigate the assassination. The Warren Commission reached two important conclusions. First, that Lee Harvey Oswald was the lone assassin. Second, that all shots that struck the president came from behind him, originating from the Texas School Book Depository where Oswald was working.

One simple way to prove a conspiracy in this case is to establish the existence of a shooter who could not be Oswald, in other words a shot that would come from the front, and exit the back of the president. There have been countless books written attempting to prove the existence of other shooters, many focusing on the witnesses in Dealey Plaza who saw someone shooting from behind a fence on the so-called "grassy knoll." I am not here to rehash that evidence. There is no need.

The existence of a conspiracy, the trump card that allows us to just prove this point, and move forward, boils down to one person: Dr. Charles Crenshaw. This man was a trained forensic pathologist who saw many gunshot wounds in his day. He was one of the many doctors in Trauma Room One to examine the president's throat wound and determine that it was absolutely a small, precise wound of entry. These types of wounds are always smaller than wounds of exit. When a bullet enters the body, it travels and carries with it human tissue to produce a larger wound of exit. This was not an exit wound. It was much too small, tight, and precise for an exit wound.

"I also identified a small opening about the diameter of a pencil at the midline of his throat to be an entry bullet hole," said

Crenshaw. "There is no doubt in my mind about that wound. I had seen dozens of them in the emergency room."[47]

Dr. Malcolm Perry also agreed with this assessment, saying to reporters that there is "an entrance wound below his Adam's apple."[48]

Because this was an entry wound, it proved that there was a person shooting from the front, in other words a man who could not be Oswald. This simple fact is all that is required to prove a conspiracy.

Making the Connection

Having proved the conspiracy let us then move forward to make the connection to the role that the Central Intelligence Agency played in this crime.

Certainly Jim Marrs' *Crossfire* and Jim Garrison's *On the Trail of the Assassins* are the authority on this matter, both exhaustively detailing the link between the CIA and the assassination. More recent developments though have shed additional light on the extent of the plot and the role of those involved.

One of the most compelling pieces of information that details the plot to kill the president comes from E. Howard Hunt. A World War Two veteran, Hunt joined the CIA in 1949, just two years after it was formed. For decades he worked in covert operations, including the failed Bay of Pigs invasion which we mentioned marked the split between JFK and the CIA. In 1973, he pleaded guilty to his role in the Watergate scandal during the Nixon administration, serving time until 1977 in federal prison.[49] He was likely in Dallas on the day of the assassination, captured in photos taken by the *Dallas Morning News* of the so-called three "tramps" taken off of a railroad car by Dallas police.[50]

When he was near death in 2006 (he eventually died on January 23, 2007) Hunt made a series of deathbed confessions to his son, St. John. Through hours of recorded conversations, E. Howard Hunt revealed the names and involvement of key members of the CIA in the assassination. Let us briefly go through them:

1. CIA Agent David Morales. Died in 1978 before he could be questioned by the House Select Committee on Assassinations. Like Hunt, he worked on the Bay Pigs Invasion fiasco, and blamed Kennedy for its failure. Recruited French assassin Lucien Sarti to be the sniper on the so-called "grassy knoll" to deliver the kill shot. Importantly Morales is a link to the southeast Asian drug trade, having served the agency both in Laos and Vietnam. He later bragged to a friend about the assassination saying, "We took care of that son of a bitch, didn't we?" Morales will be examined more in chapter three for his link to the opium trade, and two other CIA assassinations. This man took a lot of secrets to his grave.

2. CIA Agent Frank Sturgis. Worked with Hunt and other agents in covert operations in Cuba and Watergate, saying the break-in at Democratic headquarters in June 1972 was part of the cover-up of the JFK assassination. He also served as a link between the Mafia and the agency. Like Hunt, he was likely in Dallas on the day of the assassination, captured by the *Dallas Morning News* as one of the three "tramps."[51]

3. Antonio Veciana. CIA contract agent who failed in his attempt to kill Castro. Testified in front of Congress that he saw his CIA contact, David Atlee Phillips, traveling with Lee Harvey Oswald in Dallas in the summer of 1963.

4. CIA Agent David Atlee Philllips. Involved with Hunt and Sturgis in the failed Bay of Pigs Invasion. Phillips was the Mexico City CIA Station Chief when it was visited by

Oswald, who he was later seen with in September 1963 in Dallas. Recruited Veciana and Agent William K. Harvey into the plot. Went on to become CIA operations chief in Latin America where he helped to organize a successful assassination plot against a Chilean politician in 1970.

5. CIA Agent William K. Harvey. Longtime leader of clandestine operations and yet another link between the CIA and the Mafia. In 1960 he was selected to lead a covert CIA assassination team named ZR-RIFLE. He harbored bitter resentment toward JFK for his policies of peace, such as not invading Cuba, and for being demoted. Died in 1976 before he could testify in front of the House.

6. CIA Agent Cord Meyer. In charge of "Operation Mockingbird," the CIA domestic propaganda program that among other goals pushed the myth of the Domino Theory on the public. Mockingbird enlisted domestic and foreign journalists to push the CIA agenda both at home and abroad through misinformation and infiltration of various groups. As we will see in chapter three, the selling of the Domino Theory, beginning in the 1950s by the CIA, was key to convincing the public to support their various covert operations throughout the world, especially in Southeast Asia.[52] His former wife, Mary was a mistress of JFK. She was mysteriously killed in 1964. Cord Meyer was likely the group leader, coordinating the plot.[53]

Hunt said that there were more people in the agency involved, especially at the higher levels, but was unwilling or perhaps too exhausted to reveal any more skeletons in the closet, such as more about his own role. Therefore the orders to kill the president came from the highest levels of the CIA, (as we will see

Attorney General Robert Kennedy had immediately suspected this), to protect its interests in Southeast Asia regarding the Vietnam War and the opium trade. This team was given the assignment because of their proven track record to carry out assassinations, and their existing bitter hatred of the president.

The guilt of this agency is also further confirmed by the fact that now over half a century after the murder, they are still keeping secrets. Many key files that relate to the assassination have yet to be released. Here are a few key examples. According to the National Archives and Records Administration's online JFK database, the CIA still has 123 pages of files on the secret operations of William K. Harvey that they refuse to release, 606 pages of unreleased files for David Atlee Phillips, 332 pages of unreleased files for E. Howard Hunt, and 61 pages of unreleased files on David Morales.[54] As mentioned above, these are many of the key players in the assassination.

Even more frustrating is the fact that the administration of President Barack Obama declassified 175 batches of long secret government files in May 2013, but failed to release 1,100 additional pages of CIA documents that relate to the JFK assassination. The CIA says that it lacks the time and resources to review the documents, even though the documents were internally collated and secretly reviewed decades ago in 1976 in response to requests from the House Select Committee on Assassinations.[55]

The obvious conclusion here is that if there is nothing to hide, then the documents would have been released long ago. Instead, the CIA knows full well that if these files were ever publically examined it would further implicate them in the plot to kill their own commander in chief.

The definition of treason is "the offense of attempting by overt acts to overthrow the government of the state to which the offender owes allegiance, or to kill or personally injure the sovereign, or the sovereign's family."[56]

Chapter Three

The Opium Trade in Laos

Once President Kennedy reached 1963 it was becoming increasingly clear to the CIA that JFK was pursuing a broad range of policies to promote peace. He was not going to war in Laos, Vietnam, or Cuba. As we mentioned before he was seeking to end the Space Race, reduce the nuclear threat, and open more communications with the Soviet Union.

Peace would undermine nearly all that the CIA stood for. They were designed for confronting the Soviet threat, for overthrowing governments, and for making money off the opium trade in Laos, as we will see in this chapter. Kennedy's entire foreign policy was beginning to undermine their very existence.

Let us not assume that the CIA's continued existence was a foregone conclusion. Our country at that time was just beginning to experiment with having a large military during times of peace, and newly established agencies could be eliminated if the Cold War came to an end. The government disbanded thousands of agencies that were created to fight the two world wars after those wars came to an end. World War I alone had 5,000 temporary agencies.[57] In other words, it was in the interest of the CIA from a mere survival standpoint to see that the Cold War continued to exist in perpetuity.

The Cold War at that time was being fought by what were called "proxy wars" like in Vietnam or Korea. To continue this worldwide struggle between democracy and communism the American people would have to support this deadly contest of ideas. And that is where the myth of the so-called "Domino Theory" enters the equation. The Domino Theory is the idea that if one nation "falls" to communism, then the nations next to it will also become communist, and so will the ones next to that country. Pretty soon every nation will start falling like a row of dominos and they will all become communist. To stop this disease from spreading, communism must be "contained." This idea was first put forward by President Dwight Eisenhower in a press conference on April 7, 1954.[58]

Let us examine the fallacy of this theory. The United States during the Cold War was boldly proclaiming to the world that its way of life, its culture, its democracy was the best choice for all societies on earth, better than communism. This so-called Domino Theory puts absolutely no faith in democracy. It is saying that communism must be so appealing, so enticing, so dangerous, that if your neighbor gets a taste of it you will want it too. In fact, you will be overwhelmed by it. It puts no faith in the people of Southeast Asia, or anywhere else in the world, that they have right to select their own governments.

The U.S. seemed afraid that if these ignorant Asians were left to their own devices, they could never choose democracy on their own. Better to not let them see what is on the other side of that fence, or they might not think democracy is so great. If democracy truly is inherently better than communism, as the U.S. was saying, then there really would be no need to contain communism. People would naturally flock to democracy, and develop it on their own.

What this theory did was instill fear in the American people, and provide endless fodder for politicians to accuse each other of being "soft on communism." Countless elections were won and lost on who was more loyal, and who was the tougher cold warrior. The CIA and the military relied on the public to keep electing leaders like Eisenhower and Richard Nixon, one of the most voted for politicians in American history. They would support this bogus theory and the endless CIA wars, like in Southeast Asia.

The Key Players

As we move through the chronology here, four basic themes will begin to emerge. First, the CIA will begin to establish a role in the trafficking of opium in Southeast Asia. Second, President Kennedy will face enormous political pressure to invade Laos which he will resist at every turn, and in fact achieve a tenuous peace settlement for that country. Third, the CIA will attempt to sabotage JFK's policies of peace, and try various times to trick him into committing grounds troops to Laos. Such an invasion would bog down the military for years, like in Vietnam, and guarantee the continued presence of the CIA in Southeast Asia to expand the drug trade. Finally, we will examine how an extensive American military presence in Vietnam was key to the success of the trade, to provide a marketplace to sell drugs to U.S. troops stationed there.

Trying to unravel nearly a quarter century of CIA involvement in the drug trade though is no easy task. Some would say it is not even good for your health. There is of course the case of *San Jose Mercury News* reporter Gary Webb. In the 1990s he did a series of controversial articles linking the CIA to the domestic drug market. He was betrayed by his editors, forced to resign, and died mysteriously in December 2004.[59]

Before getting into the gory details of the opium trade it would be useful to make a few key points about the nation of Laos, a landlocked country next to Vietnam. Due to the climate, topography, and people, it is one of the best places in the world to grow opium, which of course gives us heroin. Laos, Thailand, and Burma form the so-called "Golden Triangle" where most of the world's opium was grown for generations.[60]

What also made this country attractive to American military commanders was the fact that the Ho Chi Minh Trail was in Laos as well. This "trail" was actually a series of supply routes that the communists in North Vietnam used to invade South Vietnam during the Vietnam War. Some in the military said that if the U.S.

could cut the Ho Chi Minh Trail then the U.S. could win the Vietnam War.[61] In 1970, Nixon's failed invasion of Laos and Cambodia to achieve this goal, proved the fallacy of this argument. JFK knew this. The U.S. military was not properly trained to fight in jungles and tunnels. The routes cut through swamps and mountains. It would not be as simple as putting up a road block on a paved road. As we will see, Kennedy refused to go to war in Laos, further angering the CIA and the military

Laos also had a civil war that raged during the 1950s and 1960s between communists and anti-communists. The names of those embroiled in this struggle for drugs, wealth, and power are unfamiliar and numerous. For simplicity's sake, and for easy reference, I have assembled a basic guide to the key players.

Four main leaders

1. General Phoumi Nosavan – U.S. backed rightist military leader installed by the CIA
2. Souvanna Phouma – neutralist
3. Prince Souphanouvong – communist half brother of Phouma
4. Kong Le – neutralist former paratrooper who briefly allied with the communists

Two primary armies

1. Pathet Lao – communist
2. Royal Laotian Army – U.S. backed army headed by Phoumi

As we begin this analysis it is important to recognize the resistance the president had to committing the U.S. military and the CIA to Laos. Very early in his administration, in fact just three months into office, it appears he had decided to work against the drug trade and war in Laos. Richard Nixon recounted in his memoirs a revealing conversation that he had with Kennedy on April 20, 1961.

"I just don't think we ought to get involved, particularly where we might find ourselves fighting millions of Chinese troops in the jungles," Kennedy said. "In any event, I don't see how we can make a move in Laos, which is thousands of miles away, if we don't make a move in Cuba, which is only ninety miles away."[62]

This was one day after the failed Bay of Pigs invasion. We mentioned before how that event marked a split between JFK and the CIA. This quote is further proof of his commitment towards peace, and it indicates that the CIA was pressuring him to go to war in Laos to make up for the fiasco that they engineered in Cuba just one day before.

The CIA had been in the opium business long before JFK even took office. In the Eisenhower administration the agency began these activities in Burma, another part of the Golden Triangle. *The New York Times* explained some of the origins of the CIA involvement in drug trafficking in an article published on April 25, 1966.

CIA agents gathered remnants of the defeated Chinese Nationalist armies in the jungles of northwest Burma, supplied them with gold and arms and encouraged them to raid Communist China. One aim was to harass Peking to a point where it might retaliate against Burma, forcing the Burmese to turn to the United States for protection. Actually, few raids occurred, and the army became a troublesome and costly burden. The CIA had enlisted the help of Gen. Phan Sriyanod, the police chief of Thailand – and a leading narcotics dealer. The Nationalists, with the planes and gold furnished them by the agents, went into the opium business.[63]

The Pressure to Invade

When President John F. Kennedy took office in January 1961, he inherited from the administration of President Dwight D. Eisenhower a complicated, unstable situation in Laos. The Geneva Accords of 1954 signaled the end of French control over Southeast Asia. The portion of these agreements which dealt with Laos called for the withdrawal of all foreign troops, a ban on Laos establishing military alliances, a limit on the types and amount of equipment that could be used by the government's Royal Laotian Army, and the creation of an International Control Commission to monitor these provisions.[64]

These conditions proved hard to enforce in Laos due to the imprecise nature of the agreements, the continued meddling of foreign nations, and the fact that the communist Laotian army, the Pathet Lao, barred the International Control Commission from getting access to the country.[65] The Soviets and the North Vietnamese continued to supply their Pathet Lao allies as various factions began fighting for control of the country.[66] In an effort to bring peace to the nation, neutralist Laotian Prince Souvanna Phouma formed a coalition government in 1957 with the help of his half-brother, Prince Souphanouvong, a communist leader allied with the Pathet Lao.[67]

The administration of President Eisenhower did not look favorably upon the coalition government. Secretary of State John Foster Dulles said that "coalitions with Communists are halfway houses to perdition," and a precursor of another "loss" to the communists.[68] Laos became a bulwark against communism and a "bastion of freedom" for Dulles.[69] CIA Director Allen Dulles hand-picked rightist General Phoumi Nosavan to lead the U.S.-backed Royal Laotian Army against the coalition government.[70] With American support, Nosavan staged a coup in 1960 which sent Souvanna into retreat with his Pathet Lao coalition allies. By supporting Nosavan, the Eisenhower Administration left Phouma with no other choice than to accept the help of

Souphanouvong, the Soviets, the North Vietnamese, and the Pathet Lao.[71]

"In this way, a local dispute in an out-of-the-way place escalated in a remarkably short period of time into a potential superpower confrontation," Kennedy administration Defense Secretary Robert McNamara wrote in 1999.[72]

Then on January 1 and 7, 1961, Pathet Lao forces joined by troops loyal to former paratrooper Kong Le scored decisive victories over General Phoumi's Royal Laotian Army.[73] Communist forces seemed on the verge of a complete takeover of the country, just days before JFK was sworn in as president on January 20.

The day prior to his inauguration, Kennedy met with President Eisenhower in the White House, along with the outgoing and incoming secretaries of State, Defense, and Treasury.[74] One of the topics on the agenda was Laos. Eisenhower told Kennedy that Laos was "the cork in the bottle of the Far East. If Laos is lost to the free world, in the long run we will lose all of Southeast Asia."[75] This was the so-called Domino Theory, and because of this, Eisenhower told the incoming president that he would "have to put troops in Laos. With other nations if possible, but alone if necessary."[76]

Kennedy aggressively responded, "If the situation was so critical, why didn't you decide to do something?"[77] Eisenhower replied that he did not feel comfortable committing ground troops with a new administration coming to power. Kennedy then asked Eisenhower's opinion on forming a coalition government in Laos, or using the American-created Southeast Asia Treaty Organization (SEATO) to provide ground troops for an invasion. Eisenhower, and his Secretary of State Christian Herter, responded that coalitions with communists would never work, and that SEATO members France and Britain would quit the alliance before sending troops to Southeast Asia.[78]

Thus Kennedy was faced with a looming problem in Laos as

he took office. The inherent character of Laos itself made it difficult for Kennedy to even consider taking military action. The landlocked, heavily forested nature of Laos, along with its many swamps and jungles made the prospects for a successful military campaign much less likely.[79] Laos is 91,400 square miles of jungle-covered mountains with tropical rain forests filled with evergreens, deciduous trees, bamboo, and scrub.[80] Much of the ground is covered with tall, tough grass.[81]

Laos also has a formidable climate characterized by two main seasons. The first season is the annual southwest monsoon, from mid-May to mid-September, which brings rain. The second season is the annual northeast monsoon, from mid-October to mid-March, which brings fog and clearer skies. In between the seasons are transitional periods of mixed weather.[82] Furthermore, the ground is often covered in smoke and haze due to slashing and burning cultivation techniques.[83] In the early 1960s (and to a large extent even today), Laos had a poorly developed road system, no railroad system, limited telecommunications capabilities, and no ports.[84] Kennedy knew that the topography, climate, and infrastructure of Laos made the chances for effective U.S. military intervention less likely.

The newly sworn in commander in chief was also faced with the fact that the army that the United States was backing in Laos was of questionable quality. For example, General Phoumi was rarely seen at the front lines of battle with his Royal Laotian Army. Moreover, his exaggerated estimates of enemy troop strength, designed to hasten U.S. intervention, served only to panic his own troops.[85]

"Phoumi is total shit," Kennedy candidly said of the general in May 1962.[86] The president knew of at least three instances when Phoumi's Royal Laotian Army had fled their positions without even telling their American military advisors.[87] Upon taking office, the new commander in chief received reports about how the Royal Laotian Army often broke ranks to pick flowers, or go swimming, one time even leaving the battlefield to join the Pathet Lao at a local festival.[88] One survey commissioned by the U.S. government in early 1961 found that approximately 90 percent of Laotians believed the earth was flat, and that they were probably the only people on it.[89]

These practical considerations were weighed against political concerns which Kennedy faced within the United States. During his campaign in 1960, Kennedy attacked the Eisenhower Administration for not challenging the communists in third world nations.[90] The possibility that he could be blamed for "losing" Laos to the communists, as Democrats had been accused of "losing" China to the communists during the Harry Truman Administration, figured into Kennedy's thinking as well.

This was certainly on the mind of many key Congressional leaders when Laos became an issue early in 1961. In February 1961, just weeks after Kennedy took office, Democratic Representative Clement J. Zablocki, chairman of the House Foreign Affairs Subcommittee on the Far East, and Representative Walter H. Judd, the ranking Republican on the committee, both urged the new president on a national radio show to not back down to the communists in Laos.

"If we show one iota of weakness there (in Laos) we are inviting trouble not only in Laos but the whole world," Zablocki said.[91] On April 7, 1961, Republican leaders Senator Everett Dirksen and Representative Charles A. Halleck were quoted in the *Washington Post* warning Kennedy not to accept any situation in Laos which would lead to a communist takeover, or suffer the political consequences.[92]

Kennedy also had military considerations to take into account as well. Late in 1960, the communist government of North Vietnam formed the National Liberation Front to bolster communist insurgency in South Vietnam with the goal of uniting Vietnam into one country under the control of the government of North Vietnam in Hanoi.[93]

As mentioned above, in order to fortify these insurgents in the south, Hanoi constructed a complex supply system known as the Ho Chi Minh Trail to provide the means to infiltrate agents, weapons, medicine, communications, machines, and troops needed to fight the war against South Vietnam.[94] This latticework of waterways, roads, and trails mostly along the course of the Annamite Mountain Chain in southeastern Laos,[95] often took up to three months to traverse along routes that were two to three feet wide, and roads eight to twelve feet wide, neither of which were usually visible from the air.[96] Many in the United States military believed that if the U.S. was to support the government of South Vietnam in their effort against the communist government of North Vietnam, the United States would have to do so in part by cutting off the Ho Chi Minh Trail, which meant invading Laos.

Against the backdrop of the conflict in Vietnam, domestic political concerns, an unreliable Laotian military ally, the Laotian climate, the Laotian topography, pressure from the Eisenhower Administration, and the complex political situation in Laos, John Kennedy began his quest for a solution to the conflict in Laos.

One of the first actions that the Kennedy Administration took in Laos was to continue the Eisenhower Administration's program of secret, CIA sponsored anti-Communist activities in Laos. The model for Kennedy's counterinsurgency policy was the 1958 book *The Ugly American* by political science professor Eugene Burdick and U.S. Navy Captain William Lederer. This book was based on events in Southeast Asia, especially Laos itself. During the 1960 presidential campaign, Senator Kennedy, along with six other prominent Americans, took out an advertisement in the *New York Times* announcing that they had sent every United States senator a copy of the book.[97]

The Ugly American was a series of fictionalized stories featuring egotistical or ignorant Americans who were outwitted by communists in their struggle to win the hearts of the people of

Southeast Asia.[98] The American heroes in the book succeeded by learning local languages and customs.[99]

"The picture as we saw it, then, is of an Asia where we stand relatively mute, locked in the cities, misunderstanding the temper and the needs of the Asians," the authors wrote in their "Factual Epilogue." "We saw America spending vast sums where Russia spends far less and achieves far more...We have been losing – not only in Asia, but everywhere."[100]

If the United States was going to beat the communists it would be among the people, on the ground.[101] To this end, at the end of February 1961 Kennedy authorized an additional $19 million to train three thousand more American advisors to practice unconventional warfare and counterinsurgency techniques in Southeast Asia, and scores of unarmed Americans using tools and books to win the hearts of Southeast Asians.[102] During this secret war in Laos, American counterinsurgents dressed in civilian clothes and had their names deleted from Defense Department rosters.[103]

The CIA also employed the Hmong in this secret war against the communists in Laos. The Hmong are an ethnic minority group in Laos who live in the northern mountains where they grow rice, corn, and opium.[104] On August 29, 1961, Kennedy, facing intense pressure, reluctantly authorized the CIA to add 2,000 more Hmong to the 9,000 man army that the agency had already organized under Eisenhower.[105] He would soon come to regret this because the agency would use these men in their secret efforts in the drug trade. The Hmong were employed by the Americans because of their tradition of rebellion and tenacious fighting, as evidenced by their successful attacks against the French during the 1920s.[106] The Hmong are also called Meo, or Miao in China, where five million Hmong live.[107] The Hmong have a 4,000 year tradition which emphasizes honor, freedom, and loyalty.[108] The Meo performed many tasks for the CIA in their war against the communists in Laos. They built airstrips by hand, kept the North Vietnamese Army and the Pathet Lao at bay, gathered intelligence, rescued aircrews, defended strategic positions, and sacrificed their men, women, and children.[109]

In return the CIA supplied the Hmong with rice, arms, and payment.[110] But there is also evidence that the CIA helped the Meo in another way. As mentioned before, Laos, Burma, Thailand, and the Yunnan Province in southern China are known as the Golden Triangle, one of the main areas in the world for growing poppy, the plant which produces opium and heroin.[111] Inadequate legislation, lax enforcement, government corruption, and high profits have made this a lucrative business for decades in the Golden Triangle. In the early 1960s, thousands of Meo depended on the opium trade for their livelihood, not to mention the fact that many smoked the drug themselves.[112]

The policy of the Kennedy Administration was to curb the flow of illegal drugs in the Golden Triangle. The CIA had something else in mind. In exchange for fighting against the communists, the CIA agreed to assist in developing the opium market in Laos.[113] One reporter for the *Far Eastern Economic Review* witnessed at Long Chieng in central Laos "American crews loading T-28 bombers while armed CIA agents chatted with uniformed Thai soldiers and piles of raw opium stood for sale in the market."[114]

One direct consequence of the CIA's actions in Southeast Asia was that because they sanctioned and supported the opium trade, the drug became readily available to U.S. troops in Vietnam and approximately 50,000 Vietnam veterans returned home to the United States as heroin addicts.[115] Kennedy eventually moved away from this counterinsurgency policy later in his administration. It will become clear why and how that happened later in this analysis.

While the CIA waged a secret war in Laos, Kennedy met with his military and political advisors to discuss American options.

Kennedy Defense Secretary Robert McNamara wrote in 1999 that four options emerged for Laos early in 1961: do nothing, do everything to crush the Pathet Lao, accept a division of Laos like Korea, or negotiate to restore a neutral government.[116] General Lyman Lemnitzer, chairman of the Joint Chiefs of Staff, advocated military intervention and disagreed with the neutrality option, citing the "vital importance of Laos to the security of the entire area and to our relations with our Southeast Asian allies."[117]

Kennedy balked at the chairman's calls for invasion partly because of Lemnitzer's own statistical analysis that the Chinese and the North Vietnamese would immediately be able to field five soldiers to every one American in the field.[118] The Joint Chiefs of Staff estimated that 60,000 American troops would be needed for a successful military intervention in Laos, plus a call-up of the reserves.[119]

Lemnitzer was not the only military advisor who called for war. Chief of Naval Operations Admiral Arleigh Burke said that if Laos was lost, the U.S. would have to send troops into South Vietnam and Thailand, arguing for a preventive war in Laos that would make clear the United States would not be forced out of Southeast Asia.[120] Army Chief of Staff General George Decker concurred with Burke, even going so far as to say that nuclear weapons should be used if necessary.[121]

The Joint Chiefs of Staff attempted to frame this debate in terms of possible lessons learned from the Korean War. They felt that a limited war with a small number of troops would guarantee defeat.[122] Many civilian advisors including McNamara and Attorney General Robert Kennedy were skeptical of the military's hawkish stance, pointing out that the Soviet Union and/or the Chinese might intervene, and the communists might easily thwart a U.S. landing at Vientiane, the Laotian capital.[123]

A New Policy for Laos

Then in February 1961 Kennedy received a letter from Prince Souvanna which indicated that Souvanna was eager to break his ties with the communists in favor of a coalition government.[124] Soon after, Kennedy felt confident to issue his first major decision on Laos. On national television on March 23, 1961, Kennedy announced the new United States policy toward Laos. The president radically changed the Eisenhower policy of supporting the goal of a "free" Laos to a new goal of supporting a "neutral and independent" Laos with a coalition government which might include communists.[125] The new president emphasized that he wanted peace, not war, through an independent Laos free of outside control brought about through discussion, not conflict. This was a dramatic departure from the Eisenhower administration's policy. Peace in Laos would spell the end of the CIA in Southeast Asia. An end to the civil war would mean the CIA would have no justification to stay in Laos, and continue their access to the drug trade.

At the same time, the president decided on a bluffing strategy designed to provoke a cease-fire, and then peace negotiations. On March 20 and March 21, 1961, he readied a Marine force in Japan, sent a 500-man unit to a helicopter base in Thailand, ordered the Seventh Fleet to steam to waters off Thailand, and directed that stockpiles of equipment and supplies be sent to the Lao-Thai border.[126]

Two events transpired in the spring of 1961 which would further convince the new president that he did not want to commit ground troops in Southeast Asia. The first was that Phoumi's army was routed by the Pathet Lao who expanded their control in the Plain of Jars region in central Laos and the eastern section of the central and southern panhandle.[127] Secondly, a group of CIA-trained soldiers were badly defeated on April 19, 1961, at the Bay of Pigs in Cuba in an effort to overthrow Cuban Communist leader Fidel Castro. The shock of Phoumi's defeat and the disaster of the Bay of Pigs Invasion left Kennedy shaken and resolutely committed to finding less confrontational approaches to solve problems within his administration, including in Laos.[128]

On April 20, the day after the fighting ended in Cuba, Kennedy had the long conversation with former Eisenhower Vice President Richard Nixon, noted above. "I just don't think we ought to get involved, particularly where we might find ourselves fighting millions of Chinese troops in the jungles," Kennedy told his former rival for the presidency. "In any event I don't see how we can make any move in Laos, which is thousands of miles away, if we don't make a move in Cuba, which is only ninety miles away."[129] On April 26, Kennedy stated that he wanted the possibility of U.S. intervention to loom as the "only card left to be played in pressing for a ceasefire."[130]

The continued threat of intervention, along with the onset of the rainy season in early May did in fact lead to a ceasefire which was announced by the Pathet Lao on May 3, 1961, and verified by the International Control Commission on May 11.[131] Negotiations began almost immediately in Geneva to work towards a new agreement on Laos. Kennedy had achieved his short term goal of garnering a cease-fire as a first step toward a coalition government for a neutral Laos. However, the president paid a political price at home for pursuing peace.

"The cease-fire in Laos came as a cold war (sic) defeat for the U.S.," *Time* magazine wrote in their coverage of Laos on May 5, 1961. "Laos...will quickly go behind the Iron Curtain...Kennedy had declared he would 'pay any price' to 'assure the survival of liberty.' But the price in Laos seemed too high."[132]

Despite this criticism, Kennedy was able to achieve a major diplomatic breakthrough on Laos when he met with Soviet Premier Nikita Khrushchev for a summit in Vienna, Austria, in June 1961. The two leaders agreed to seek a neutral and independent Laos together, free of either American or Soviet influence. A joint statement issued at the end of the summit read "The President and the Chairman reaffirmed their support of a neutral and independent Laos under a government chosen by the Laotians themselves, and of international agreements for insuring that neutrality and independence, and in this conjunction they have recognized the importance of an effective ceasefire."[133]

Both leaders agreed that a neutral Laos, and perhaps later even a neutral Southeast Asia, was a better alternative to a larger sphere of Chinese influence in the area.[134] Officials in the Kennedy Administration came to power with the notion that China was an unpredictable and aggressive nation, as shown by their intervention in the Korean War.[135] A Chinese takeover of Southeast Asia would damage America's credibility and present Chinese communism as an attractive, cutting edge alternative to non-aligned nations.[136] Kennedy felt that Beijing might have designs on expansionism, an idea that JFK explained to the Soviet leader would be just as unattractive from the Soviet perspective.[137]

Throughout the late summer and autumn of 1961, Kennedy continued to receive pressure from his advisors to invade Laos. On July 28, 1961, National Security Council Advisor Robert Johnson pressed Kennedy for a contingency plan for invasion in case the ongoing negotiations in Geneva failed. The president angrily responded that the negotiations should be carried on in good faith, and that he was "very reluctant to make a decision to go into Laos. Nothing would be worse than an unsuccessful intervention in this area."[138]

Nonetheless, the Chairman of the Joint Chiefs of Staff General Lyman Lemnitzer, along with the help of Secretary of Defense McNamara drew up unilateral American invasion plans for Laos, against the president's wishes.[139] On October 1, 1962, the Joint Chiefs issued a grim report to Kennedy saying that the time had passed when actions short of a full scale military invasion "could reverse the rapidly worsening situation...There is no feasible military alternative of lesser magnitude which will prevent the loss of Laos, South Vietnam, and ultimately Southeast Asia."[140]

Kennedy also began to receive conflicting advice about the importance of the Ho Chi Minh Trail. On October 5, 1961, a special national intelligence estimate indicated that only a small part of the insurgents in South Vietnam came from outside that country and reported little evidence that they relied on external supplies.[141] However, the next month General Maxwell Taylor, special military representative to Kennedy, returned from a mission to South Vietnam urging the president to help Diem organize a border force to close the Ho Chi Minh Trail.[142] Then in December 1961, the State Department weighed in on the issue with a paper documenting numerous cases of communist men and military material moving into South Vietnam via Laos.[143]

Yet Roger Hilsman, director of the Bureau of Intelligence and Research at the State Department, offered a conflicting view of the importance of the trail after his own visit to the country the following year. Hilsman issued a report to Kennedy with the help of Michael Forrestal, a presidential aide, which read in part: "Thus the conclusion seems inescapable that the Viet Cong could continue the war effort at the present level, or perhaps increase it, even if the infiltration routes were completely closed."[144] This report basically told the president that even if 60,000 men fought and died to close those invasion routes, the war would continue anyway.

Faced with pressure from his advisors, and conflicting information on the Ho Chi Minh Trail, Kennedy continued to resist calls for an invasion of Laos.

Averell Harriman, chairman of the U.S. delegation to the ongoing Geneva peace negotiations on Laos, recognized that the military situation presented a potential pitfall. If General Phoumi learned that the United States military had drawn up contingency plans for invasion, even without the president's approval, he would have little incentive to negotiate for peace.[145]

The CIA Digs In

Harriman was also deeply concerned about the level of resistance against Kennedy's new policy toward Laos. Harriman complained that the State Department was clinging to the policies of the Eisenhower Administration and refusing to recognize the "radical changes in policy which the new administration has introduced"[146] in Laos. Robert Amory, deputy director of the CIA, pointed to scores of people at the State Department and the CIA who were opposed to Kennedy's efforts toward peace including the following: Assistant Secretary of Defense Paul Nitze, Joint Chiefs of Staff aide Victor Krulak, Deputy Assistant Secretary of Defense William Bundy, CIA Operations Chief Richard Bissell, CIA Director John McCone, and the entire staff of the International Security Affairs Office.[147]

Kennedy and Harriman used a number of strategies to work around this resistance. First, Harriman arranged to have CIA Agent John Hasey removed from Laos in early 1962. Harriman knew that Hasey, a close friend of Phoumi's, was deliberately trying to subvert the peace process.

The second strategy was to suspend aid from General Phoumi in an effort to get him to go to the negotiating table. The United States was providing on average about $20 per person to the two million people of Laos during Kennedy's Administration, which was about twice as much per capita as any other country.[148] The president decided to suspend a portion of this aid on two separate occasions as a negotiating tool. On January 7, 1962, the State Department started holding back its monthly payment of $4 million to the U.S.-backed Royal Laotian Government headed by Boun Oum, who had refused to negotiate with Phouma and Souphanouvong in Geneva.[149] Just four days later Oum agreed to negotiate and American aid was resumed within 48 hours.[150]

However, in February, Oum continued to remain obstinate by refusing to allow neutralists to occupy the ministries of defense and interior in a proposed coalition government. Kennedy responded by cutting off the money which paid the salaries of General Phoumi's army.[151] Phoumi and Oum continued to hold out, realizing that Washington could not afford to seriously cripple their strength, lest they provide an open path for the Pathet Lao to take over.

Phoumi also had a backup plan. He had always been the darling of the CIA since the Eisenhower Administration. He was hand picked by the agency to be a Laotian cabinet minister in February 1959 and named a general the following year. At that point Phoumi had been knee deep in bringing opium into Laos from neighboring Burma with the help of the CIA. With the agency's help he staged rigged elections, killed opponents, and recruited a formidable army to ostensibly "fight communism" while assisting the CIA in trafficking heroin. With JFK's insistence on stopping the drug trade, working with neutralists and cutting Laotian aid, this forced the CIA and Phoumi's government to turn even more to the opium trade to fund Phoumi's government. By the time the early 1960s arrived Laos had become the opium capital of the world. The Laotian Opium Administration, the Laotian prime minister, and the CIA were all in on the fun with Phoumi, including developing a seedy gambling casino in downtown Vientiane.[152]

But it would soon become clear how far the CIA would go in trying to force the Kennedy administration to make a greater commitment to Laos. An invasion of Laos would provoke a wider war in Southeast Asia. This would require a huge commitment of ground troops, perhaps 60,000 men as mentioned above. More war means more covert operations which equals greater access to the drug trade and more American GIs to sell the opium to. Just as one example, the month that the president died in November 1963, 1,146 kilos of raw opium were shipped from Laos to South Vietnam, netting $97,410 profit for the CIA and Phoumi.[153]

In 1961, the president was convinced that the CIA had deliberately caused the Bay of Pigs Invasion to fail to trick him into going to war with the Soviet Union. Instead he refused to invade Cuba, and a second time the following year during the Cuban Missile Crisis. The agency was up to its old tricks again in the spring of 1962. A plan was put forward to try to trick the president to commit ground forces to Laos by destroying the very army that the CIA had helped to create. This major event was the Battle of Nam Tha in May 1962.

Nam Tha was a northwest provincial capital in Laos, twenty miles from the Chinese border. General Phoumi had been building up his forces at Nam Tha for several months before the battle "in an effort to alter the balance of power in northwestern Laos," according to a *New York Times* report on May 7.[154] Seven or eight weeks before the battle, the Kennedy administration told Phoumi, according to the *Times*, "in the most forceful terms that the extensive buildup would invite an attack,"[155] but the warnings went unheeded. Such a buildup during the rainy season was unthinkable because Phoumi would be unable to supply and reinforce his troops in the event of an attack.[156]

On May 5, 1962, 5,200 men in Phoumi's Royal Laotian Army were routed at Nam Tha as many fled to Thailand or the Chinese border in a state of panic as the communist Pathet Lao army completed their victory.[157] The *New York Times* cited several unnamed sources in the Kennedy Administration who "indicated the opinion that the Royal Laotian forces had provoked the attack on Nam Tha,"[158] but they did not understand why.

Just a few days later, on May 16, 1962, *The Times* (of London) offered a provocative explanation for the debacle at Nam Tha. The article stated that the Central Intelligence Agency was behind the defeat in an effort to force the Kennedy Administration to intervene with U.S. ground forces, or face defeat in Laos. "C.I.A. agents in Laos deliberately opposed the official American objective of trying to establish a neutral Government," the article stated. The CIA "encouraged General

Phoumi Nosavan in the concentration of troops that brought about the swift and disastrous response of the Pathet Lao."[159]

Furthermore, the article offered an explanation as to why Kennedy's suspension of aid had not forced Oum and Phoumi to accept neutralists into the coalition government. The *Times* (of London) stated that "the agency provided them (Oum and Phoumi) with some funds from its own capacious budget."[160] This article makes sense in light of the expulsion of CIA agent John Hasey, as noted above, and the intense opposition to Kennedy's policy on Laos, noted earlier as well.

In the other words, the CIA risked a complete communist takeover of Laos, and the destruction of the army it helped to create to try to force the president to go to war in Southeast Asia. And not only that, the agency was secretly neutralizing the effect of JFK's withdrawal of aid by giving Phoumi money from its own budget, and money from the opium trade. This was a complete betrayal and subversion of the president's policy of peace and neutrality, with the single purpose of provoking war to continue their access to the opium trade.

This plan of sabotage by the CIA and Phoumi backfired on them drastically. Kennedy still refused to invade Laos, and Phoumi and Oum were both left powerless. As long as they had an army in the field they could resist U.S. pressure to join a coalition government. Now that their army was either in ruins or on the run, they were forced to salvage what they could through negotiation.

However, Kennedy still had to deal with a now more powerful Pathet Lao army. To this end he once again turned to military bluffing, using the threat of intervention as a means to negotiation. He dispatched the Seventh Fleet to the Gulf of Thailand and sent U.S. troops to the Thailand-Laos border.[161]

Another factor in securing a peace settlement was secret talks between Kennedy and Khrushchev through intermediaries. On May 22, 1962, Attorney General Robert Kennedy met with Soviet intelligence officer Georgi Bolshakov.[162] Through this meeting, Khrushchev communicated to Kennedy that he could guarantee a stoppage in further military action on the part of the Pathet Lao if Kennedy agreed to call back American troops from the Thailand-Laos border. Kennedy told his brother to tell Bolshakov to communicate to the Soviet leader that the pullback would begin in ten days, which it did. The Pathet Lao called off their offensive.[163]

With the communist army subdued, with Phoumi and Oum in line, and with Khrushchev in step with Kennedy, the situation was never more ideal for a new peace accord to be reached on Laos. In Geneva on July 23, 1962, representatives from fourteen nations signed the Declaration on the Neutrality of Laos.[164] This agreement called for a neutral, non-aligned Laos, the withdrawal of all foreign troops, the prohibition of foreign interference in the Laotian government, permission for Laos to establish diplomatic relations with other countries, and the stipulation that foreign aid should be given to Laos and accepted by Laos unconditionally.[165] Under the Protocol to the Declaration on the Neutrality of Laos, which was also signed that day by the same 14 nations, an International Control Commission was set up to monitor the provisions of the accords.[166]

Most importantly however, the new peace accords created a coalition government which included the three competing factions in Laos, the communists, the neutralists, and the American-backed rightists. Souvanna Phouma, a neutralist, became Prime Minister, while Boun Oum, the American-backed anti-communist, and Prince Souphanouvong, a communist, were made cabinet members.[167] Kennedy was disappointed that the agreement had failed to unify the armies, which he felt was a key step toward a long term peace. Nonetheless, the American president hailed the agreements as a "significant milestone in our efforts to maintain and further world peace."[168] He reflected a personal feeling of satisfaction when he said that "it is a heartening indication that difficult, seemingly insoluble international problems can in fact be solved by patient diplomacy."[169]

Kennedy had high hopes for these peace accords. "Kennedy was always looking for opportunities to see if we could expand from the Laos agreements," said William Sullivan, Harriman's assistant throughout the Geneva negotiations.[170] Kennedy looked to expand the neutrality of Laos throughout all of Southeast Asia. He instructed Harriman and Sullivan to search out the prospects for such a goal while in Geneva.

At the successful conclusion of the Geneva Conference on Laos on July 23, 1962, Kennedy instructed Harriman to meet in secret with Chinese Foreign Minister Chen Yi to discuss the idea of a regional neutralization of Southeast Asia. The Chinese said that this was not possible until the issue of Taiwan was resolved to the satisfaction of Beijing.[171] A Chinese border war with American ally India in October 1962 further ended any prospect for American cooperation with the Chinese.[172]

Kennedy also had Harriman meet with North Vietnamese Foreign Minister Ung Van Khiem, on July 23, the day of the signing.[173] The meeting resulted in an exchange of charges and countercharges between the two sides, and went "absolutely nowhere," according to Sullivan, who attended the meeting.[174]

Despite these setbacks, Kennedy had hope for the future of Southeast Asia. After the conclusion of the Geneva Agreements on Laos, Under Secretary of State George Ball called for an "independent belt" in Southeast Asia to include Cambodia, Vietnam, Burma, Thailand, Laos, and Malaya as part of a "Presidential Peace Charter for Southeast Asia."[175] Roger Hilsman, director of Intelligence and Research at the State Department, said Kennedy "accepted the concept as a far seeing expression of the ultimate goal for Southeast Asia."[176]

In accordance with the terms of the new accords, the American president began the withdrawal of all U.S. military personnel in Laos. Between July 23, 1962, when the agreements were signed, and October 7, the deadline to withdraw all foreign personnel, Kennedy withdrew 666 military advisors from Laos.[177] The only American military presence that remained in Laos were the guards at the United States embassy at Vientiane, the capital.[178] By December 1962, photographic reconnaissance sorties over Laos were terminated as well, after a combined 720 flights over Vietnam and Laos between 1961 and 1962.[179] What makes these moves even more impactful is that they came less than a month after the president issued NSAM 55, 56, and 57, in which he severely neutered the ability of the CIA to operate independently, and dramatically curtailed their ability to stage covert operations. He was making good on his promise to splinter the CIA into a thousand pieces. Nevertheless, as we will see below, they would fight back against this effort to remove them from Southeast Asia.

CIA Sabotage

The president was very proud of his continued efforts toward peace and freedom throughout the world. In fact he made it one of his themes in his final state of the union address delivered on January 14, 1963. "In the world beyond our borders, steady progress has been made in building a world of order. The people of West Berlin remain both free and secure. A settlement, though still precarious, has been reached in Laos,"[180] JFK said. Later in the speech the president seemed hopeful that his efforts at peace would be received well by the communists.

If they come to realize that their ambitions cannot succeed, if they see their "wars of liberation" and subversion will ultimately fail, if they recognize that there is more security in accepting inspection than in permitting new nations to master the black arts of nuclear war...then, surely, the areas of agreement can be very wide indeed: ...stability in Southeast Asia, an end to nuclear testing, new checks on surprise or

accidental attack, and, ultimately, general and complete disar-
mament. For we seek not the worldwide victory of one nation
or system but a worldwide victory of man. The modern globe
is too small, its weapons are too destructive, and its disorders
are too contagious to permit any other kind of victory.[181]

The Kennedy Administration insisted on sticking by the Laotian
peace agreement, thus ending its support for CIA counterinsurgency in Laos. Roger Hilsman, Kennedy's Director of the Bureau
of Intelligence and Research at the State Department, said that
the ties were cut completely to Laos, except for some airdrops.
"It was only after Kennedy was killed and we (some Kennedy
advisors, including Hilsman) were kicked out and Johnson came
in and started bombing (North Vietnam) that all the contacts
with the Meo were reactivated."[182]

The first few months after the signing of the new peace agreements were crucial months and Kennedy knew it. General
Phoumi was of particular concern considering his history of
causing problems for the administration. Phoumi had to support
the coalition, but the proper amount of pressure had to be
applied to keep him in the fold.

"We can't afford to squeeze Phoumi so hard in the next three
or four months because, as I say, we've got so much to lose if that
were to ever go south," the president said on August 21, 1962 at
a White House meeting. "We don't want to press him too hard
until we see a clearer path. The next six months is critical."[183]

Unfortunately, throughout the rest of Kennedy's presidency
the coalition government in Laos began to crumble. One reason
was the continued presence of thousands of North Vietnamese
troops who continued to supply and embolden their communist
Pathet Lao allies. The Pathet Lao then made an attempt to win
outright control of the government by trying to win over the
neutralists to its side. Although this attempt largely failed, it
caused a rift in the government after which the Pathet Lao broke

its ties to the neutralist army headed by Kong Le.[184]

By early 1963, skirmishes broke out between the Pathet Lao and the neutralist army. On April 1, 1963, any hope for the success of the coalition government ended when Foreign Minister Quinim Pholsena was assassinated after the Pathet Lao murdered one of Kong Le's neutralist officers.[185] The Pathet Lao withdrew its representatives from the government, signaling the end of the coalition government which lasted less than one year.[186]By the end of April 1963, open warfare returned to the country as the Pathet Lao attacked the strategic Plain of Jars in northern Laos, a high plateau dotted by stone jars holding the ashes of the dead.[187] The Plain of Jars was important to all sides because it overlooked the Ho Chi Minh Trail used to supply communists in South Vietnam.[188]

There was more to this story though that was happening behind the scenes. April 1963 was the month when the CIA tried to undo all that JFK had worked for in Laos. Even though the thousands of military advisors had been withdrawn as noted above, the CIA defiantly refused to leave the country, supported by their own Congressionally-approved secret "black budget," plus money garnered from the opium market. They were going to see to it that the neutralist government was going to fail, and that war would return to Laos. The first step was to assassinate Foreign Minister Quinim Pholsena, one of the fair minded progressive diplomats JFK was counting on to hold the tenuous coalition government together.

Author Wilfred Burchett paid a visit to Laos in April 1963 to report on the "swarms of CIA agents" who were planning what amounted to an "Iranian style military coup."[189] The first step in the agency's plan was to assassinate Pholesena.

"On April 1, Quinim Pholsena, head of the 'Peace and Neutrality' party, comprising progressive forces among the neutralists, was shot down as he walked up the steps of his Vientiane home after attending a Royal reception," Burchett reported in May 1963. "His wife, a political figure in her own right, was severely wounded in the assassination." After she recovered a few days later, Pholsena's wife told him she had "no doubt" that the assassins were from the CIA.[190]

The next step for the agency was to provoke war in the strategic Plain of Jars, as noted above, by attempting to desta-bilize Kong Le's neutralist forces, by infiltrating them with men loyal to CIA puppet Phoumi. "By the second and third week of April, Nosavan's battalions started moving up towards the Plain of Jars, the gates opened for them in some places by the infil-trators among Kong Le's troops," Burchett said. "The assassi-nation of Pholsena was the signal for a brutal assault on progres-sives. With tanks and armored cars patrolling the Vientiane streets, scores of progressives were hunted down and arrested,"[191] by the CIA.

This was yet another example of the CIA deliberately trying to undermine the president's policies of peace. As with the battle of Nam Tha, the CIA was again trying to engineer a return to war in Laos that would continue to justify their presence there. Predictably, the Joint Chiefs of Staff once again renewed their calls for an invasion of Laos, offering Kennedy four options with which to invade. Ultimately, Kennedy rejected all four options, one month after he had already angered the Joint Chiefs by rejecting Operation Northwoods. Every spring the president had to beat back the war hawks. First it was the call to invade Cuba in April 1961, then to invade Laos in May 1962 after the Battle of Nam Tha, and again when the CIA attempted "an Iranian style military coup," in May 1963. Each time the president held his ground, to the increasing frustration and anger of the Central Intelligence Agency.

A further escalation in tensions happened when an American aircraft in Laos was shot down on September 5, 1963, killing pilot-in-command Joseph Cheney, and co-pilot, Charles Herrick, both Americans. The rest of the passengers were from Thailand,

and they managed to parachute to safety but were eventually captured by the Pathet Lao.[192] The official version of these events in the media was that the communists shot down the plane, but in reality, was this one final chance for the CIA to provoke an invasion? Can we ever really know who shot down that aircraft?

A number of aspects to the story do seem a bit unusual. The plane was an Air America C-46, owned and operated of course by the CIA. Everyone and everything on that aircraft was expendable. The two pilots were not CIA agents, but instead were civilian sub contractors, who therefore could be easily sacrificed and manipulated by the agency. It is likely in fact that Merrick and Cheney did not even know what they were getting into, thinking they were working for Pacific Corp., never knowing that this was in fact a CIA front company based in Thailand, but in reality was Air America. During their brief time working for the agency, they were probably told to go from point "a" to point "b" and not ask any questions about who was on the plane, or what they were transporting, such as opium.

Merrick and Cheney had been flying missions for less than a year. In fact, this was only their fourth run. Perhaps one of the men had seen too much, and started asking questions about who really owned Pacific Corp, or what they were really transporting. Maybe on one of their previous runs they transported drugs against their will. Equally possible is that Merrick or Cheney may have seen other pilots shipping opium and they knew it would just be a matter of time until they would be required to do so as well. Merrick was a decorated veteran of both World War Two and the Korean War. Both were married men, and Merrick was a father of two who was born in Buffalo, New York, an unlikely fit for an international drug runner. Both families were never told for decades that the two pilots were being subcontracted to work for the CIA. The agency was equally disinterested for decades in looking for their remains, which were not returned to the United States for nearly 40 years. A rescue mission was attempted two days later, but further examination of the site was mysteriously "overruled" by the U.S. embassy in Laos.

The obvious assumption here is that the shooting down of this aircraft served two purposes for the Central Intelligence Agency. First, the communists would get blamed for it. This would lead to yet another call for an invasion of Laos that the CIA desperately wanted, to ensure years of access to the drug trade, and of course a wider base to sell their heroin to more American GIs. Second, these expendable men may have been assassinated to silence them, if they were asking too many questions. Merrick's daughter, Gayle Herrick Holt, in fact indirectly seemed to question how it was that all the other passengers were able to parachute to safety and not her father, and Cheney. "Did he really not get a chance to jump out?" she inquired to a *Washington Post* reporter in 2003 when her father's remains were interred at Arlington National Cemetery.[193]

The cargo on the plane was also expendable. This time, Cheney and Merrick were only transporting rice and meat, not the valuable opium that was on so many other Air America transports. In other words, if this aircraft had opium on board that was selling for over $1,000 per kilo, and was being piloted by actual CIA agents, men who been in the agency long enough to make themselves anything but expendable, would this crash have ever occurred?

Keep in mind as well that because this was an Air America C-46, the CIA would also know the flight path, and be able to position itself where they wanted with anti-aircraft fire to take down the plane. It is standard CIA protocol to enlist other elements, or assign blame to other entities in the name of getting the job done. For example, the agency has often employed the Mafia in many of its assassination plots, such as those planned for Fidel Castro. In other words, it is also possible that the CIA may have enlisted the Pathet Lao to execute this plan, and assign blame to them. It would not have been the first time they would have helped them out. Their actions in regards to the battle of Nam Tha prove that they were willing to help the communists for the greater goal of provoking war. Something just does not seem right about this story. In the final analysis, we are left with more questions than answers with this tragic incident for the families of those two men.[194]

Whether this event was coordinated by the CIA or not, the Joint Chiefs of Staff and Kennedy's national security advisors predictably renewed calls for an attack. This would mean that these men wanted the U.S. to commit 60,000 ground troops to avenge the loss of two lives lost on one American aircraft that the CIA could not even publically claim was owned by their agency. JFK didn't bite, still finding the military choices "unpalatable." He remained steadfastly committed to not violate the terms of the Geneva Accords throughout the remainder of his time in office.[195] He would have just over two months left to live.

In retrospect it seems quite remarkable that this young president could so consistently stick to his policies of peace. In fact, his thinking on Laos should inform historians who still continue to doubt his insistence on peace in Vietnam. Both situations were very similar and the president saw nothing but disaster if the U.S. made broad commitments to these places half way around the world where the geography and ground conditions made military success nearly impossible.

Equally remarkable is the treasonous actions of the CIA who at least twice (that we know of) at the Battle of Nam Tha, and in April 1963, tried to trick the president to invade Laos. Remember that a military commitment to Laos would mean a force of 60,000 troops that would bog down the U.S. in Laos for years to come, in other words a second Vietnam War while the one we all know about would be raging next door for an endless number of years as well. A wider Southeast Asia War with the Chinese involved may have quickly begun. It would be in the interest of the CIA to keep these wars going in perpetuity to ensure that the agency had access to the drug trade, and a huge marketplace of troops in Laos, and in Vietnam to sell heroin to. An invasion would also allow the agency to keep pushing the need to contain communism while fighting for the myth of the Domino Theory, while in reality they could continue trafficking drugs. Their first foray into this deadly game of cat and mouse with the president was to destroy the anti-communist army to force JFK to invade Laos to "save it" from "falling" to communism. Their second effort to provoke this incursion was the plot hatched in April 1963 to cripple JFK's peaceful neutralist government, which would bring war back to Laos, and renew calls for an attack. War did return, but Kennedy still did not invade. A last attempt may have been made in September 1963 when an American aircraft was suspiciously shot down in Laos just two months before his assassination. Still the president would not move off his policies of peace, and cutting all ties to Laos. The CIA had other ideas, one of which of course, as we explained in the previous chapter, was to assassinate President John F. Kennedy.

The Vietnam Connection

We also mentioned in the previous chapter that by the end of 1963 the president had decided to end the Vietnam War. This would be horrible news for the CIA. This has often been cited as a motive for only the military to want the president dead. Military leaders wanted war for Cold War reasons, national pride, and profit. The president's policies of peace were against those ideas. All that is true, but the link to Laos and drugs has yet to be made. A war in Vietnam was essential to the continued opium trafficking in Laos. Presidents Johnson and Nixon expanded the Vietnam War and therefore allowed for the continued presence of the CIA in Southeast Asia, and the continued beating of their hearts. If the war ended, the CIA would be forced to leave, no longer being able to force feed the Domino Theory to the public. But if the war could continue, the drug trade could too. And most importantly the agency could sell heroin to American GIs in Vietnam. These men were willing customers, seeking relief from the intense combat and post traumatic stress disorder that they suffered from.

"The sudden burst of heroin addiction among GIs," notes historian Alfred W. McCoy, "was the most important development in Southeast Asia's narcotics traffic since the region attained self-sufficiency in opium production in the late 1950s." With the help of the CIA, by 1969 "the Golden Triangle region was harvesting close to one thousand tons of raw opium annually, exporting morphine base to European heroin laboratories, and shipping substantial quantities of narcotics to Hong Kong both for local consumption and re-export to the United States."[196]

One of the primary CIA markets was not just Laos but in Vietnam as well, where street peddlers and road side stands offered the drug for sale to American troops. Even after the American soldiers were dead, they were still useful to the CIA who would often split open corpses, and stuff them with up to 50 pounds of heroin to be shipped home. Conspiring CIA agents back in the United States took out the drugs from the corpses to then be distributed to the domestic marketplace.[197]

A president who wanted to end the Vietnam War would cause serious problems for an agency so intent on making a killing off of the opium trade. Laos and Vietnam are linked together in this. The CIA wanted drugs and war in Laos, and did all they could to establish that with their own money and with subterfuge as we chronicled in the previous section. Despite enormous pressure, the president angrily pushed back, never committing to war in Laos or Vietnam. And with Vietnam, the CIA needed that as an open market for eventually half a million potential customers who were in desperate need of some kind of relief from the horrible guerrilla warfare that typified that quagmire. Although this may not have been the only motivating factor, it provided a powerful incentive on the part of the high command within the Central Intelligence Agency (who were deeply involved and informed on all Southeast Asian covert operations) to remove a commander in chief who they refused to take orders from. With Kennedy out of the way, the drug trade in Laos, and the war in Vietnam could expand beyond the wildest hopes and dreams of the CIA. And as we will see, that is exactly what happened, as drug addicts and millions of Asians died in their wake.

Johnson and Nixon Cast Their Lots

Much to the delight of the CIA and the military, President Lyndon Johnson and President Richard Nixon both saw to significant expansions of the Vietnam War, which ensured that by extension a greater commitment would be made to Laos as well, all in the name of fighting the Cold War communist threat. Just four days after JFK's assassination, the newly sworn in president approved National Security Action Memorandum 273.

"It remains the central objection of the United States Government in South Vietnam to assist the people and government of that country to win their contest against the externally directed and supported communist conspiracy," the document read. This essentially reversed Kennedy's withdrawal policy, documented in chapter two. "The test of all U.S. decisions and actions in this area should be the effectiveness of their contribution to this purpose." President Johnson also said that he expected "full unity of support" throughout the entire government for this new policy, perhaps expecting some resistance from Secretary of Defense Robert McNamara, or other JFK appointees. LBJ also approved the planning for any necessary "increased activity" for the CIA, the Department of State, and the Department of Defense in point number seven. Importantly, point eight on the memorandum approved for more covert operations into Laos to address the "fluctuating situation."[198]

It would only be when Johnson was in the last days of his

administration, when he was a lame duck president with nothing to fear, that he made an attempt to end the war. However, the 1968 peace conferences were sabotaged by the next president of the United States, the GOP Nominee, Richard Nixon. Journalist Robert Parry of *Consortium News* wrote an article about this on May 8, 2013.

In late October 1968, Beverly Deepe, a 33-year-old Saigon correspondent for the *Christian Science Monitor*, came upon a story that could have changed history. A six-year veteran covering the Vietnam War, she learned from South Vietnamese sources that Richard Nixon's campaign was collaborating behind the scenes with the Saigon government to derail President Lyndon Johnson's peace talks.

On Oct. 28, Deepe sent her startling information to her *Monitor* editors in the United States, asking them to have the Washington bureau "check out a report that [South Vietnamese Ambassador to the United States] Bui Diem had sent a cable to the Foreign Ministry about contact with the Nixon camp," she told me in a recent e-mail exchange.

At that moment in 1968, the stakes surrounding Nixon's secret contacts could hardly be higher. With half a million U.S. soldiers serving in the war zone – and with more than 30,000 already dead – a peace deal could have saved countless lives, both American and Vietnamese. Progress toward a settlement also could have meant defeat for Nixon on Election Day, Nov. 5.

The peace talks would eventually collapse, embarrassing Vice President Hubert Humphrey, the Democratic nominee, as well as President Johnson who secretly called Nixon's actions "treason." Nixon of course extended the Vietnam War for nearly four more years, expanding it into Laos and Cambodia as well. Thus even before he became president, Nixon was making it clear that he was on the side of the CIA and the military, and had no interest in ending the war, or changing the status quo.[199] With Kennedy out of the way, and two presidents interested in flexing their Cold War muscles, opium trafficking in Southeast Asia would see a decade of expansion, with the CIA right in the middle of the action.

The Drug Trade Expands

In 1966, the CIA appointed Theodore Shackley to be the head of their secret war in Laos. Thomas G. Clines was named as Shackley's second in command. Agents Carl E. Jenkins, David Morales, Raphael Quintero, Felix Rodriguez, and Edwin Wilson were also sent by the CIA to assist Shackley in Laos. According to the reporting of Israeli journalist Joel Bainerman, Shackley and his appointed teammates immediately joined in on the existing CIA opium trade. Their go-to guy was General Vang Pao.[200]

General Pao was ostensibly yet another leader of the anti-communist forces in Laos, but in reality Pao was a major figure in Southeast Asian drug trafficking. Shackley used his CIA contacts and assets to eliminate any competitors, giving Vang Pao and the CIA a monopoly over the heroin market in Laos. In 1967, Zieng Khouang Air Transport Company was formed. This was Vang Pao's own airline which Shackley and Clines provided the funds for to create an easy way to transport opium and heroin between Long Tieng, Vientiane, or anywhere else there was a market for the drug, like in Vietnam.[201]

In 1968, Mafia kingpin Santo Trafficante and General Pao met in Saigon to establish a more efficient heroin-smuggling operation from Southeast Asia to the United States. The meeting was arranged by Shackley and Clines, according to historian Alfred McCoy.[202]

CIA agent David Morales was appointed by Shackley to take

charge of a black operations base designed to focus on paramilitary action within Laos. The base was located in Laos at a city called Pakse, and was used to harass the Ho Chi Minh Trail and kill anyone who worked against the CIA drug operations. To this end, when Shackley became Station Chief in Vietnam, he and Morales established the Phoenix Program, which entailed the killing of civilians suspected of being communist. Within two years, Operation Phoenix liquidated 28,978 civilians in Vietnam and Laos, many of whom were seeking to undermine CIA influence in Southeast Asia.[203] Though officially established in 1969, such activities were taking place long before that year.

Let us not forget that this David Morales is the same David Morales that E. Howard Hunt named as one of the key agents who conspired to assassinate President Kennedy. What' an amazing coincidence. We will meet him again in the next chapter, as we explore his link to other CIA assassinations. Of all the people involved in the JFK, RFK, and MLK assassinations, his name seems to come up the most in connection to all three assassinations. Morales was known to be a hard drinking, ruthless operative. Of all the secret CIA files on the assassination, the ones that relate to Morales might provide the most insight. I would imagine that the 61 pages of documents that are still sealed on this man will never see the light of day, or if so would be severely redacted.

One has to suspect that Operation Phoenix, which Morales helped to coordinate, may have had a more nefarious goal as well. We saw in Laos that the CIA would do nearly anything to keep the civil war going there, including destroying the anti-communist army to force an invasion, or wreck the peaceful neutral government to create a climate of war. Operation Phoenix was probably designed to keep the Vietnam War going as long as possible, to keep it rising from the ashes, to keep Johnson and Nixon satisfied with body counts and optimistic reports of a war that was allegedly on the verge of success. Or perhaps if the tide was turning towards American victory, do whatever it took to turn the tide back to extend the war. In reality, the CIA was doing more drug trafficking than fighting the communists.

The CIA's personal charter airline, Air America, was key to this. "Air America was known to be flying Meo opium as late as 1971. Meo village leaders in the area west of the Plain of Jars, for example, claim that their 1970 and 1971 opium harvests were bought up by Vang Pao's officers and flown to Long Tieng on Air America UH-lH helicopters," reported historian Alfred McCoy in 1972. The opium was "destined for heroin laboratories in LongTieng or Vientiane, and ultimately, for GI addicts in Vietnam."[204]

With the CIA increasingly entrenched in Laos and Vietnam, thanks to Johnson and Nixon who both expanded and continued the Vietnam War for years, anyone who stood in the way of the CIA staying in Southeast Asia also had to be eliminated. In the mid to late 1960s there were three very powerful voices who were calling for radical changes in America's pro-drug and pro-war policies. They were Malcolm X, Dr. Martin Luther King, and Robert F. Kennedy. As we will discover in chapter four, all three of these men were assassinated by the Central Intelligence Agency. It is time to understand why.

Chapter Four

Trinity of Death: Connecting the Malcolm X, MLK, and RFK Assassinations

Having demonstrated that the CIA would stop at nothing to see the opium trade in Southeast Asia continue and flourish, the logical question would be just how far they would go to keep this drug trafficking flourishing in perpetuity. We have already seen sabotage, assassinations, and subterfuge as parts of their game plan, but after JFK's death, three other significant threats emerged to the continued existence of the CIA, and the unrelenting flow of drugs out of the Golden Triangle. These three threats were Malcolm X, Martin Luther King, and Robert Kennedy. As with the JFK assassination, we will briefly establish the complicity of the CIA in these assassinations. Then we will proceed to examine how the policies, statements, and followers of these men posed serious threats to the Central Intelligence Agency. Let us begin with Malcolm X, a man who ironically enough spent a large portion of his life as a drug dealer, and a substance abuser.

"I'm not at all sure it's the Muslims"

There is no need to rehash the entire history of Malcolm X, but needless to say he was one of the most important leaders in African American history. Here was a man who had gone through a series of dramatic changes throughout the course of his short life. His father Earl Little, a member of Marcus Garvey's Negro Improvement Association, was brutally executed by the Ku Klux Klan when Malcolm was just a child. This young man quickly turned to a life of crime that included gambling, prostitution, and drugs. His time in jail was transformational as he turned to God, becoming a devout Muslim and a member of

Elijah Muhammad's radically pro-black Nation of Islam. Over time he developed into an effective preacher with a strong following as he proclaimed a doctrine of African American self defense and black pride.

In 1964, Malcolm X made a pilgrimage to the Islamic holy city of Mecca in the Middle East which radically changed his perspective. He began to see that not all white people are evil and he charted another new course, talking about the "brotherhood" of man "under one God." His break from the Nation of Islam caused great anger and jealousy within its ranks when Malcolm X took many of its followers with him to found a new organization called the Organization of Afro-American Unity. He visited many world leaders in Africa as well, and at the end of his life he was seeking to combine forces with Martin Luther King. Their common ground was Malcolm X's idea to enlist the support of African leaders in the struggle for black pride and power. Many of these politicians were very receptive to this idea and Malcolm X's additional goal to bring up the issue of African American rights in front of the United Nations. Malcolm X wanted to charge the U.S. with human rights violations in front of the world court. This would be a huge embarrassment to the United States in its Cold War contest of ideas with the Soviet Union. It might undermine the entire premise of the Cold War. Suddenly he was becoming even more powerful, and more of a threat. Within months of his return from Africa, with a return visit already in the works, Malcolm X was assassinated while speaking at the Audubon Ballroom in New York City, on February 21, 1965. This was only fifteen months after the JFK assassination.[205]

Untangling the evidence that the CIA played a central role in the assassination of Malcolm X is no easy task, and like the JFK assassination, it is also apparently not good for your health. In the late 1960s, television news reporter Louis Lomax got the idea about doing a movie exploring the life of Malcolm X. Earlier in his career he had teamed up with another young reporter named Mike Wallace to do a series on Malcolm X and the Nation of Islam that was titled "The Hate that Hate Produced." It began airing on June 13, 1959. Lomax maintained an interest in the black Muslim leader over the years, and a few years after Malcolm X's death, he felt motivated to begin producing a full length feature film about the life and death of this powerful black leader. The main focus of the script was how the Central Intelligence Agency played a primary role in his assassination. Unfortunately, this movie never made it to the big screen. Lomax died on July 31, 1970, when his car crashed. His brakes had been cut. He was on his way to the production studio at the time of this deadly "accident."[206]

The illegal harassment, surveillance, and bombing of his own home lead Malcolm X to conclude that the Nation of Islam, which he had recently broke away from, could not be responsible for all the constant threats to his life. "The more I keep thinking about this thing," he told author Alex Haley, who was helping him write his autobiography, "the things that have been happening lately, I'm not at all sure it's the Muslims. I know what they can do, and what they can't do, and they can't do some of the stuff recently going on."[207]

At the time of Malcolm X's death, he was already being closely monitored on a nearly hour to hour basis by the FBI Director, the CIA Director, the CIA's Deputy Director of Plans (responsible for covert actions and assassinations), the Director of Naval Intelligence, the Chief of the Air Force Counterintelligence Division, and the Army's Assistant Chief of Staff for Intelligence.[208] This was essentially the entire intelligence apparatus of the federal government.

There are two incidents that have the markings of the CIA all over them. The first one happened on July 23, 1964, just seven months before his slaying. The black leader was in Cairo, Egypt, to address the Organization of African Unity Conference, and present a petition seeking cooperation in his effort to bring U.S.

human rights violations before the United Nations. The night before his scheduled speech, Malcolm X was having dinner at the Nile Hilton Hotel in Cairo with members of his entourage that included New York City Councilman Milton Henry. Malcolm X and Henry noticed two white men sitting nearby watching them eat. They had been trailing the black leaders all day. "There was one agent who especially irritated Malcolm," Henry said. "We couldn't eat without him being at the next table."[209] Suddenly Malcolm X got violently ill. "He would have died," Henry said, "if we had not been able to get him to the hospital in a hurry."

At the hospital, doctors immediately pumped the stomach of Malcolm X. The contents were sent for analysis. The results proved that someone had placed a "toxic substance" in the food of the Black Muslim leader. The doctor insisted that the chance that the food was naturally tainted by something like botulism was "nil." An attempt was made to find the waiter who served them, but he mysteriously disappeared. "Someone deliberately tried to poison me," he said. It would not have been the first time the CIA tried to poison a world leader. Other examples of CIA poisoning plots included Cuban dictator Fidel Castro throughout the 1960s, Congo leader Patrice Lumumba in 1960, and Chinese Premier Chou En-lai, at the Afro-Asian Conference in Bangdung, in 1955.[210]

Despite the poisoning, Malcolm X submitted his petition to the conference anyway, and received widespread support to "internationalize the American Negro problem so as to accentuate the struggle," he said. "This can only be done by linking the fate of the new African states with that of the American Negroes."[211] He also pledged to form a coalition with Martin Luther King to speak as a single voice on African issues. Nothing was going to stop Malcolm X in his struggle for justice, except death. This was becoming increasingly clear to the CIA. Even Malcolm X knew he was a marked man, saying "I will never get old."[212]

This leads us to the second incident that seemed to have a frightening impact on this Black Muslim leader. He began to realize that there were very powerful forces out to get him. It happened just 12 days before his assassination. "The more I keep thinking about what happened to me in France," he told Alex Haley, "I think I'm going to quit saying it's the Muslims."[213]

On February 9, Malcolm X flew to Orly Airport in Paris for a speaking engagement, but was immediately surrounded by French police and barred entry to the country. He was forced to fly back to London and eventually back to the United States where death awaited him just a few days later. Malcolm X was confused by this because he had just spoken in France three months before, and France was a democracy with a free press. It made little sense to treat him like a criminal. In April 1965, an investigative journalist named Eric Norden, who was researching the Malcolm X assassination, received the answer as to why this Black Muslim leader had been denied admission into Paris. The person who he received this information from chose to remain anonymous, likely for his own safety. Norden was told by a powerful African diplomat that his country's intelligence agency "had been quietly informed by the French Department of Alien Documentation and Counter-Espionage that the CIA planned Malcolm's murder, and France feared he might be liquidated on its soil." French intelligence had passed this information to the diplomat because his north African country had been one of the many nations that Malcolm X had just completed a successful visit to. French agents knew that after being denied entry into Paris, the black leader might choose to go back to that north African country. If that happened, French intelligence advised that north African nation to be ready for the CIA to try to carry out another plot against his life on African soil.[214] Such an attempt by the CIA had already been tried once before on that continent six months earlier. It is interesting to note that France would feel compelled to issue this warning in an apparent attempt to save his life, but not afford him any measure of their own security that he could have received if they allowed him to enter France. Nevertheless, word was likely getting around within the various intelligence communities in Europe and Africa that according to this anonymous African diplomat, the "CIA is beginning to murder its own citizens now."[215]

Historian and investigative reporter James W. Douglass summarized the situation best when he said "Malcolm realized that...the Nation of Islam was now serving as a proxy, much like how the CIA used the Mafia as their go-between in the attempted killing of Castro." The use of hired NOI assassins in the shooting of Malcolm X, (most of whom escaped the crime scene and have never been identified), "furnished a plausible deniability and a showy scapegoat," Douglass wrote. This was a counterintelligence operation planned at high levels of our government, a "joint FBI-CIA operation, (and) the Nation of Islam was being used as a religious Mafia."[216]

An Early Opponent of the Vietnam War

Having established the CIA's role in the assassination, the motivation to kill this Black Muslim leader was due to two primary factors. The first was his intense and early opposition to the Vietnam War, and the second was his effort to end the use of drugs within the African American community. Malcolm X was a powerful voice advocating against the use of drugs. His commitment to living a drug-free life was an influential example to countless other African Americans. He could speak from authority, knowing first-hand the dangers of drug abuse from his early life. A leader like this could undermine the entire African American marketplace that the CIA and the Mafia were using to sell drugs to. His opposition to the war was also another factor in the motivation to assassinate him. A continued war in Vietnam meant constant access to the drug trade, and a marketplace for heroin in Vietnam. Malcolm X was easily the most powerful and influential voice within the Civil Rights Movement who condemned both drugs and the Vietnam War, the two things held most dearly by the Central Intelligence Agency. This could not be tolerated.

In retrospect it seems anachronistic that any major public figure would be commending the Vietnam War in 1965 (when Malcolm X was assassinated), or even years earlier. Traditionally, historians associate opposition to the war with the late 1960s, when widespread public protesting began after the American public watched gruesome images of their soldiers dying on the streets of Vietnam in January and February 1968, during the Tet Offensive. With this in mind, the criticisms of the war that Malcolm X was making would seem that much more courageous and prescient on his part, given the early nature of them, and dangerous from the perspective of the CIA. In fact, as early as 1954 when the CIA first got involved in Southeast Asia, Malcolm X was comparing the suffering and plight of the oppressed in Vietnam with those of black Americans.[217]

Later in his life, as the war intensified during the Johnson administration, his attacks sharpened. On April 3, 1964, at a rally in Cleveland, Ohio, Malcolm X issued a scathing attack on the futility of fighting an unwinnable guerilla war in Southeast Asia, a lesson not learned until years later by the American military.

> The dark people are waking up. They're losing their fear of the white man. No place where he's fighting right now is he winning. Everywhere he's fighting, he's fighting someone of your and my complexion. And they're beating him. He can't win any more…. The white man can't win another war fighting on the ground. Those days are over. The black man knows it, the brown man knows it, the red man knows it, and the yellow man knows it. So they engage him in guerrilla warfare. That's not his style. You've got to have heart to be a guerrilla warrior, and he hasn't got any heart.

It takes heart to be a guerrilla warrior because you're on your own. In conventional warfare you have tanks and a whole lot of other people with you to back you up – planes over your head and all that kind of stuff. But a guerrilla is on his own. All you have is a rifle, some sneakers, and a bowl of rice, and that's all you need, and a lot of heart.

People who just a few years previously were rice farmers got together and ran the heavily-mechanized French army out of Indochina. You don't need it – modern warfare today won't work. This is the day of the guerrilla... Algerians, who were nothing but Bedouins, took a ride and sneaked off to the hills, and de Gaulle and all of his highfalutin' war machinery couldn't defeat those guerrillas. Nowhere on this earth does the white man win in guerrilla warfare...Just as guerrilla warfare is prevailing in Asia and in parts of Africa and in parts of Latin America, you've got to be mighty naive, or you've got to play the black man cheap, if you don't think some day he's going to wake up and find that it's got to be the ballot or the bullet.[218]

The following year he continued his assault on the war in the weeks before he was assassinated. "It shows the real ignorance of those who control the American power structure. If France, with all types of heavy arms, as deeply entrenched as she was in what was called Indochina, couldn't stay there. I don't see how anybody in their right mind can think the U.S. can get in there. It's impossible," Malcolm X said in 1965. "So it shows her ignorance, her blindness, her lack of foresight and hindsight; and her complete defeat in South Vietnam is only a matter of time."[219]

A strange aspect to his anti-war stance was the fact that police found a North Vietnamese stamp inside of his address book that he was carrying on him at the time of the assassination. The circa 1965 stamp depicts two North Vietnamese guerilla warriors with rifles attempting to shoot down an American helicopter. Why he was carrying this stamp, what it meant to him, and where he got it from are the subjects of much debate. It does however add one more bizarre aspect, and more unanswered questions, to his assassination.[220]

"The White Man's Poison"

If any person could speak powerfully about the dangers of drug use, it would be Malcolm X. He admitted to Alex Haley that he had abused marijuana, cocaine, Benzedrine, tobacco, alcohol, and ironically opium, that was probably brought to the United States by the CIA.[221]

The use of drugs and alcohol ("the white man's poison"[222]) was strictly prohibited by members of the Nation of Islam, and Malcolm X typically laced his sermons with a powerful anti-drug message. "We turn to drugs because we're trapped. We turn to drugs and alcohol seeking an escape from the hell that the white man has trapped us in here in America," he said. "We're trapped. We know no way out, so we get a wine bottle, we get a whisky bottle, or we stick a needle in our arms, or we smoke pot, trying to find an escape from the hell the white man has given us for 400 years here in America. So this is a false escape."[223]

On June 24, 1964, Malcolm made a major speech in Harlem at the Audubon Ballroom introducing the country to his newly formed Organization of African Unity.[224] He would be assassinated in less than a year speaking at that very same spot. He lectured for well over an hour about his new vision of African and African American unity. He also made one his most scathing attacks yet on the dangers of drug abuse.

"So our purpose is to organize the community so that we ourselves, since the police can't, eliminate the drug traffic, we have to eliminate it. Since the police can't eliminate organized gambling, we have to eliminate it," Malcolm X said. The speech was a call to arms for his followers, and an indictment of the New

York City Police Department. "Since the police can't eliminate organized prostitution and all of these evils that are destroying the moral fiber of our community, it is up to you and me to eliminate these evils ourselves."

Later in the speech the OAU leader made one his most famous statements on drug addiction, and its impact on the family unit. "Drug addiction turns your little sister into a prostitute before she gets into her teens; makes a criminal out of your little brother before he gets into his teens," he said, drawing from his own life experiences. "And if you and I aren't men enough to get at the root of these things, then we don't even have the right to walk around here complaining about it in any form whatsoever. The police will not eliminate it. Our community must reinforce its moral responsibility to rid itself of the effects of years of exploitation, neglect, and apathy, and wage an unrelenting struggle against police brutality."

Malcolm X also saw plenty of blame for the drug trade within the government, for allowing drugs to penetrate and infect urban centers. "When a person is a drug addict, he's not the criminal; he's a victim of the criminal. The criminal is the man downtown who brings drugs into the country. Negroes can't bring drugs into this country. You don't have any boats. You don't have any airplanes. You don't have any diplomatic immunity," he said near the end of his speech. "It is not you who is responsible for bringing in drugs. You're just a little tool that is used by the man downtown. The man that controls the drug traffic sits in city hall or he sits in the state house. Big shots who are respected, who function in high circles those are the ones who control these things."

There was also a call to action that Malcolm X included in his address, laying out an organizational structure for the OAU. He made a strong appeal for members who would help with basic jobs like having a newspaper for the group, taking action to the streets, and providing better education for African Americans so they can move away from a life of drugs and repression. "And you and I will never strike at the root of it until we strike at the man downtown," he said. "We must create meaningful, creative, useful activities for those who were led astray down the avenues of vice."

Chillingly, Malcolm X closed the speech by taking a shot at former CIA Director Allen Dulles, saying "this man can find a missing person in China. They send the CIA all the way to China and find somebody. They send the FBI anywhere and find somebody. But they can't find them whenever the criminal is white and the victim is black, then they can't find them."[225] It was a strange tangent about Dulles who at that point was working on the Warren Commission, which had yet to release its findings on the Kennedy assassination.[226] This seems like a statement that he may have added in extemporaneously for reasons known only to himself. One month later the CIA would try to kill the OAU leader in Egypt after making this speech laced with his powerful anti-drug messages.

The Drug Connection

The first person to suggest that Malcolm X was killed because of the international drug trade was a man named James Farmer. It is interesting to connect some various pieces to this puzzle, to follow some lines of evidence to bring us back to Farmer's suggestion about the drug connection.

James Farmer was a friend and colleague of the Black Muslim leader, and a fellow well known member of the Civil Rights Movement. Farmer founded the Congress of Racial Equality (CORE), and was the organizer of the famous CORE Freedom Ride in 1961 that protested the segregation of public transportation.[227] Farmer told the *New York Times* that Malcolm X had been killed for speaking out against the use of drugs within the African American community. He hinted that the slaying had "international implications" and was organized by the drug trafficking industry, which at that time was controlled by the Mafia and the CIA.[228]

Malcolm X's lawyer, Percy Sutton agreed with this assessment, saying, "Jim, I don't know whether you realize how right you were in what you said about Malcolm's murder. Furthermore, I understand the smart boys in Harlem are wondering how you could know so much from the outside."[229] The "smart boys" in Harlem had been fooled into thinking that the assassination was solely an operation planned and executed by the Nation of Islam. Farmer knew better.

In fact, even the Nation of Islam had connections to the international drug trade, perhaps introduced to them by the CIA or the Mafia. Elijah Muhammad's son, Nathaniel, was arrested and convicted for drug distribution in the Midwest in 1975. This followed the involvement of members of a New Jersey mosque who were linked to a series of drug related murders in 1973.[230]

However, there is much more to the James Farmer aspect to this story. How exactly did Farmer know that there were international drug implications to the assassination? Who told him? In 1997, veteran investigative journalist Danny Schechter did his own digging into CIA activities in Africa. In the 1960s he did some reporting for *Ramparts* magazine in San Francisco that exposed covert CIA funding of college organizations. Schechter was based in the London bureau of the magazine at the time and was given the Africa beat. He was able to uncover hundreds of groups that were on the CIA payroll in Africa. He discovered "a covertly mobilized, multilayed, Cold War apparatus… shrouded in a system based on plausible deniability."[231] He discovered hundreds of journalists on the CIA payroll who would send back to the American people "a steady stream of anti-communist propaganda designed to stoke our fear of the red menace."[232] This is the myth of the Domino Theory again being pushed, this time in Africa though, not Southeast Asia.

Schechter went further and became interested in following

the CIA money trail in Africa. He found many leaders who were rented to serve various political purposes. Eventually, in 1968, this hard working reporter founded the Africa Research Group "to oppose the nefarious web of covert political warfare, counterinsurgency, and the support of repressive regimes in the name of democracy,"[233] the very legacy of the CIA in Africa. Along the way, Schechter was able to raise some serious questions about CIA activities in Africa, based on his extensive networks of sources. He essentially concluded for example that Nelson Mandela was in jail because of a tip by a CIA agent given to the South African police, and that the CIA assassinated Patrice Lumumba of the Congo. Then he dropped a bombshell, probably without even knowing.

Schechter discovered that the CIA had dispatched James Farmer to Africa to "challenge Malcolm X's growing influence there,"[234] and he wanted to know why. It seems fairly certain that by the summer of 1964 and into the winter of 1965, word was getting out in Africa that the CIA was plotting to kill this new leader that many Africans were increasingly falling in love with. Eric Norden was told as much in April 1965 by a high ranking north African diplomat. And then of course there was the CIA assassination attempt on Egyptian soil in July 1964. Africans were very well versed in CIA meddling. They knew when they were involved in these plots to kill various leaders, such as Lumumba of the Congo. The CIA often promoted one leader over another, choosing to lift Moise Tshombe to power by assassinating Lumumba, for example.[235] At the time, Farmer was repudiating the growing activism and militancy of the CORE, thinking it was moving away too quickly from non-violence.[236] It is likely that the agency was choosing the much less militant James Farmer as their point man in Africa, to undermine the influence of Malcolm X, as Schechter concluded. Farmer would be briefly contracted to go to Africa to fill the void once the assassination took place, and calm any anger that might be directed towards Americans in that continent. In fact, Farmer was placed in Africa the month of the assassination, February 1965. There is plenty of evidence that this is exactly how the CIA planned it.

First of all, Farmer was able to avoid assassination, unlike King and Malcolm X, living to the age of 79 when he died in 1999.[237] Secondly, it would not be unheard of for the CIA to enlist, however briefly, an infiltrator into its ranks. Malcolm X himself was approached to be a government informant in 1955, but he told the agents to "go back to hell."[238] Third, and most importantly, Farmer was informed of the assassination three weeks before the shooting took place, and it seems he did very little to stop it. On February 1, 1965, Farmer was in Ghana visiting with Prime Minister Kwame Nkrumah. During his stay in Ghana he had dinner with an American political activist whom he had met in New York City many years ago. She was now living in Ghana for some unknown reason. The conversation turned to Malcolm X.

"He is going to be killed, you know," she said. Then she told him when, and she was not wrong. "He will be killed sometime between now and April 1."[239] He never relayed this information to his supposed "friend," Malcolm. Farmer probably knew a lot more than he let on. If he indeed was working for the agency, as Schechter suspected, it would make sense that he would be informed when the assassination was going to take place. Was Farmer briefly contracted to be in Africa to be ready to fill the void of Malcolm X, to step into the power vacuum it created for him, and/or simply calm any feelings of anger among the African people?

It also makes perfect sense that, later in his life, Farmer began to back away from his statements that there was a CIA drug connection to the assassination. As we said before, saying such things can be bad for your health. Interestingly, the year after the assassination, Farmer resigned from CORE and left the Civil Rights Movement entirely, later becoming of all things a member of Republican Richard Nixon's administration.[240] What a radical departure this was from his earlier "freedom riding" days. Was this simple disillusionment on his part, or a case of doing what needs to be done to survive, having seen first-hand what happens to those who speak out too loudly?

A Malcolm X and King Coalition?

What may have been even more frightening to the CIA than Malcolm X's anti-drug and anti-war stance was the possibility that he might join forces with Martin Luther King. If these men had a unified voice on drugs and war, despite their other differences, they would be an unstoppable force for change. The possibility of some kind of cooperation between the nation's two foremost civil rights leaders was becoming more of a reality in 1964 and into 1965.

The first and only time the two men met was on March 27, 1964, when they were listening to the debate in the Congress over the proposed Civil Rights Bill. King made some provocative statements (made even more impactful with Malcolm X standing at his side) saying that if the bill was not passed by the first week of May, King would seek to persuade the Congress "at first with our words," as he paused for effect, "then our *deeds*." King added ominously that if the bill is not passed "our nation is in for a dark night of social disruption."[241]

Malcolm X then began to form a coalition of seventeen civil rights groups known as ACT. It was based out of New York City and called for a peaceful twenty-four hour school boycott in six major cities if the U.S. Senate did not end debate on the proposed Civil Rights Bill by May 5, Dr. King's deadline. Quietly, a number of the branches of King's Southern Christian Leadership Conference (SCLC) were members of ACT.[242] This provided an important and tangible bond between the two leaders. More were coming.

Other links between King and Malcolm X included attorney

William R. Ming who was legal counsel to both the Nation of Islam and Martin Luther King,[243] as well as Alabama civil rights activist Slater Hunter King (a cousin of Martin Luther King) who negotiated land deals with Malcolm X in 1961.[244]

Also, when Malcolm X formed his Organization of African Unity in the summer of 1964, he explicitly said that he would make every effort to form a coalition with King, and other prominent civil rights activists. On June 27, 1964, Malcolm X was informed via a phone call from King's lawyer Clarence Jones that Dr. King was interested in helping Malcolm X get his human rights petition in front of the United Nations.[245] This was a major moment in the life of Malcolm X. With King's support, it looked like he was finally going to be able to achieve unprecedented levels of change for his growing anti-drug, anti-war, and black-empowering Organization of African Unity.

One month later the CIA would make its first attempt to assassinate Malcolm X. The second time they would not fail, and leave the world wondering what might have been if these two leaders could have continued on their paths towards each other, and cooperation. The CIA was not going to let that happen. Soon they would begin planning to assassinate Dr. King as well.

Regicide: Connecting the King Assassination

We have already established in chapter two the importance and lucrative nature of the drug trade in Laos to the CIA, and the equally essential heroin marketplace in Vietnam. President Kennedy's assassination served to eliminate his resistance to both sides of this equation and usher in an expansion of CIA drug trafficking and war throughout the 1960s and early 1970s under Johnson and Nixon. However, as the 1960s began to move forward, two very powerful men posed serious threats to the continued existence of the drug trade, and the Vietnam War. They were Martin Luther King, and Robert F. Kennedy. Both of these men would be eliminated within months of each other by the Central Intelligence Agency in the spring of 1968. King was poised to begin a broad based "Poor Peoples' Campaign,"[246] complete with a march on Washington to demand more policies to help the nation's impoverished, be they black or white. He was ready to begin this new phase in his life when he was struck down by a single assassin's bullet at 6 p.m. on April 4, 1968, in Memphis, Tennessee, while standing on the balcony of the Lorraine Motel. He was there to support a sanitation workers strike. The official version is that James Earl Jay, a racist ex-con, was the lone killer, which of course is far from the truth.

"The CIA ordered it done"

Untangling the role of the CIA in the assassination of Martin Luther King is no easy task, and some would say it is not even good for your health. When Congressman Walter Fauntroy, (a former King associate) began exploring the idea of writing a book to explore these connections, he began to feel threatened by the Justice Department so he quickly told them, "I won't go finish the book, because it's surely not worth it."[247]

1968 was a key year for the expansion of drugs in Southeast Asia and the United States. CIA agents Ted Shackley and Thomas G. Clines, arranged a key meeting in January of that year in Saigon. The meeting was between Mafia kingpin Santo Trafficante, and Laotian drug runner/CIA puppet Vang Pao. The purpose of this little get together was to establish a more efficient heroin smuggling operation between Southeast Asia and the United States.[248] The continued involvement of the U.S. in Laos and Vietnam would be essential to the success of this plan so the CIA could remain "to fight communism" while also continuing to run the drug trade. This was a presidential election year, and Martin Luther King and Robert Kennedy were denouncing the war on an almost daily basis. Within months they would both be silenced by the CIA.

The connections between the CIA and the Mafia are

widespread and widely known, such as with the drug trade and planning assassinations together. To summarize the findings of decades of investigation by attorney William Pepper, he essentially concluded that on April 4, 1968, there were two teams of assassins ready to take out MLK in Memphis. One was controlled by the local Memphis Mafia with help from the Memphis police department. The other was a trained CIA/military team waiting as a backup plan at a remote location in case the first team failed. The Mafia "assassination operation provided the government with a plausibly deniable alternative to the use of its own trained professionals who were waiting in the wings and ultimately not required," Pepper said. Organized crime "insulates federal, state, and public officials...from responsibility for a variety of illegal acts. The underlying financial arrangements...rarely come to light." The assassination of King was a "searing indictment of betrayal and abuse of power."[249]

Pepper also uncovered a strange conversation that a barbershop worker named Bill Hamblin overheard in the Cherokee Barbershop in Memphis about two weeks after the assassination. His boss, Vernon Jones, had a customer in the shop who was an FBI agent named Purdy. This man was a client of Jones for going on ten years. According to Hamblin, Jones asked Purdy as he was leaving that day who killed Martin Luther King. The agent's response was, "the CIA ordered it done."[250]

It makes sense that the FBI would know that the CIA was involved. Congressman Fauntroy as he was leaving office in 1991 read some secret FBI files on the King assassination. They basically said that FBI Director J. Edgar Hoover in the weeks before the assassination had a series of meetings "with persons involved with the CIA and military intelligence in the Phoenix Operation in Southeast Asia."[251] The backup assassination team had been drawn from the CIA's Phoenix Operation. Author Douglas Valentine who wrote a book on the Phoenix Program in 1990 confirmed that the men from the program were redeployed into the Army's 111th Military Intelligence Group that was in Memphis on April 4 to photograph the assassination and provide backup assistance if the Mafia ordered plot failed. CIA agent Jack Terrell later confirmed this under oath saying that his CIA friend J.D. Hill was a member of the sniper team, but was later mysteriously shot dead.[252]

It is essential to note that the assassins came from the Phoenix Program. This program was designed to keep the Vietnam War going as long as possible as we mentioned before, and it was laced with agents who were also deeply involved in the opium trade like Ted Shackley, who oversaw the Phoenix Program, and David Morales who he appointed to run the day to day operations of it. This ties the King assassination directly to the opium trade. It is also interesting to note that Morales was of course one of the men who E. Howard Hunt pinned as being one of the main conspirators in the assassination of President Kennedy. Was he a member of the King sniper team as well? It seems possible that Shackley may have ordered this assassination, recommended it, or suggested possible assassins from his team. The topic may even have been brought up during the meeting he arranged between Trafficante and Vang Pao that took place just months before the killing. Shackley had been in Vietnam and Laos since 1965, so operations akin to the Phoenix Program were probably taking place long before 1968. Another possibility is that the agency may have informed Shackley that the assassination was in the works and to proceed with the meeting as one part of an overall plan for actions in 1968 that included the Mafia meeting, the King assassination, and the Robert Kennedy assassination. As we will explore later in this chapter, the Phoenix Program is directly connected to RFK's slaying as well through of all people, David Morales.

"The Greatest Purveyor of Violence in the World"

Like Malcolm X before him, one of the most vocal and early

opponents of the Vietnam War was Dr. King. He was a persistent and thoughtful critic of America's war policy that from his perspective was wasting time, money, and lives, while essentially holding back America from aiding its own people. As we will see, his voice of protest grew stronger and more influential in the late 1960s, much to the frustration of the CIA who were counting on the public to keep absorbing the lies of the Domino Theory, and that of a winnable war in Southeast Asia to allow the CIA to continue its drug trade.

Just over a month after the assassination of Malcolm X, on April 1, 1965, in Baltimore, Maryland, Dr. King expressed his opinion at an SCLC executive board meeting that he and his fellow activists needed to start being more critical of President Johnson's Vietnam policy. The following January he published a critical attack on the Vietnam War, which helped convince the executive board of the SCLC to officially condemn the war a few month later.[253]

In the spring of 1967, at Riverside Church in New York City, Reverend Martin Luther King spoke for well over hour about a single topic: the evil that the Vietnam War was doing to the United States. He spoke passionately and from his soul, saying that his campaign to uplift America's poor people was directly tied to ending the Vietnam War, that as long as the war continued, and money and lives were sacrificed, then Lyndon Johnson's so called war on poverty could never be won.

"I could never again raise my voice against the violence of the oppressed in the ghettos without having first spoken clearly to the greatest purveyor of violence in the world today – my own government, " King said. "For the sake of those boys, for the sake of this government, for the sake of the hundreds of thousands trembling under our violence, I cannot be silent."[254] King spoke of Vietnam as a mistake, as madness, and a nightmare that needed to end immediately.

Somehow this madness must cease. We must stop now. I speak as a child of God and brother to the suffering poor of Vietnam. I speak for those whose land is being laid waste, whose homes are being destroyed, whose culture is being subverted. I speak for the poor of America who are paying the double price of hopes at home, and death and corruption in Vietnam. I speak as a citizen of the world, for the world as it stands aghast at the path we have taken. I speak as one who loves America, to the leaders of our own nation: The great initiative in this war is ours; the initiative to stop it must be ours.[255]

The reverend called for an immediate end to the bombing of Vietnam, a complete withdrawal of troops, and a start to real peace negotiations. The nation's foremost civil rights leader seemed to suggest that he was also aware of the CIA's drug trade when he said, "If we continue, there will be no doubt in my mind and in the mind of the world that we have no honorable intentions in Vietnam." In fact, Dr. King directly called for an end to the drug trade by saying that the U.S needs to "take immediate steps to prevent other battlegrounds in Southeast Asia by curtailing our military buildup in Thailand and our interference in Laos."[256] This speech was the strongest condemnation of the Vietnam War that King had made in his life.[257]

In the intervening year, Rev. King kept up his assault on American war policy. Later that month on April 30, 1967, at the Ebenezer Baptist Church in Atlanta, Georgia, he said "I oppose the war in Vietnam because I love America. I speak out against this war, not in anger, but with anxiety and sorrow in my heart, and, above all, with a passionate desire to see our beloved country stand as the moral example of the world. I speak out against this war because I am disappointed with America " said Rev. King. "We are presently moving down a dead-end road that can lead to national disaster."[258]

In August 1967, he continued his theme of tying the war to economic injustice. "John Kenneth Galbraith said that a guaranteed annual income could be done for about twenty billion dollars a year," the civil rights leader said. "And I say to you today, that if our nation can spend thirty-five billion dollars a year to fight an unjust, evil war in Vietnam, and twenty billion dollars to put a man on the moon, it can spend billions of dollars to put God's children on their own two feet right here on earth."[259]

On Christmas Eve, 1967, he delivered a sermon saying, "Every time we drop our bombs in North Vietnam, President Johnson talks eloquently about peace. What is the problem? They are talking about peace as a distant goal, as an end we seek, but one day we must come to see that peace is not merely a distant goal we seek, but that it is a means by which we arrive at that goal." Ironically, one of the most destructive, gruesome battles of the Vietnam War, the Tet Offensive, would begin the following month. "We must pursue peaceful ends through peaceful means. All of this is saying that, in the final analysis, means and ends must cohere because the end is preexistent in the means, and ultimately destructive means cannot bring about constructive ends."[260]

These attacks on the injustice of the war would not end until his life ended on April 4, 1968, exactly one year after he made his first major speech condemning the war on April 4, 1967, at the Riverside Church, in New York. Surely a coincidence.

The Final Hope: The Robert F. Kennedy Assassination

After the assassinations of JFK, Malcolm X, and Martin Luther King, many in the Civil Rights Movement turned to Robert Kennedy as their last, best hope for real change to help the working poor, and to end the Vietnam War. RFK's campaign for the presidency in 1968 was largely centered on the ideas of healing racial tensions, lifting up the working class, and ending the Vietnam War, making him another target of the CIA.

Even before he became a candidate for the presidency, Robert Kennedy was speaking out against American war policy. He made a speech on February 8, 1968, in Chicago, that condemned the Vietnam War, and called for an immediate end to combat operations. "Unable to defeat our enemy or break his will – at least without a huge, long and ever more costly effort – we must actively seek a peaceful settlement," he said. "The best way to save our most precious stake in Vietnam – the lives of our soldiers – is to stop the enlargement of the war, and that the best way to end casualties is to end the war."[261]

One problem that he faced though in his efforts to capture the Democratic nomination for the presidency was the fact that he joined the campaign fairly late, announcing his intention to run on March 16, 1968. However, he made it perfectly clear why he was running, and what changes would be coming if he became president.

"I run because I am convinced that this country is on a perilous course and because I have such strong feelings about what must be done," Kennedy said, a U.S. Senator from New York. "I run to seek new policies – policies to end the bloodshed in Vietnam and in our cities, policies to close the gaps that now exist between black and white, between rich and poor, between young and old, in this country and around the rest of the world."[262]

Later in his announcement speech, RFK went further in his attack on the military and the CIA, who by March 1968 were firmly entrenched in Southeast Asia, and were less than 3 weeks away from killing Martin Luther King.

"In private talks and in public, I have tried in vain to alter our course in Vietnam before it further saps our spirit and our manpower, further raises the risks of wider war, and further destroys the country and the people it was meant to save," Kennedy said, standing in the same room that his brother announced for the presidency in 1960, the Senate Office Building. "I cannot stand aside from the contest that will decide our nation's future and our children's future."[263]

Drawing on his time as attorney general under JFK's administration, Senator Kennedy said that his experience during many times of crisis "taught me something about both the uses and limitations of military power, about the opportunities and the dangers which await our nation in many corners of the globe in which I have traveled."[264] Importantly, RFK made a point to say that one particular lesson he learned about the limitations of military and its dangers was during "the negotiations on Laos."[265] This likely signaled an intention on his part to restore the peace agreement in Laos that his brother had worked so hard to achieve. This would be horrible news for the CIA, on top of the fact that Kennedy would immediately end the Vietnam War if elected president. Such talk of "limitations of military power" was probably not well received at CIA headquarters.

Just two days later he continued his assault on the Vietnam War at a lecture given on March 18, 1968, at Kansas State University. "I am concerned that, at the end of it all, there will only be more Americans killed; more of our treasure spilled out; and because of the bitterness and hatred on every side of this war, more hundreds of thousands of Vietnamese slaughtered; so that they may say, as Tacitus said of Rome: 'They made a desert, and called it peace.'"[266]

His campaign moved through the spring as he battled Minnesota Senator Eugene McCarthy and Vice President Hubert Humphrey for the Democratic nomination for the presidency. Kennedy would need a victory in the California primary on June 5, 1968, to overcome McCarthy's delegate lead to have a good chance to secure the nomination. The winner of this state would capture all of the delegates from California. RFK beat McCarthy 46% to 42% that night, and secured an easy victory in South Dakota, 50% to McCarthy's 20%. All told it was a big night for the

New York State senator.[267] Another sign of hope was that his own state of New York, with another huge trove of delegates still had yet to hold their primary, scheduled for June 18.[268] Most importantly, in August the Democratic convention was going to be held in Chicago, a city run by Kennedy stalwart Mayor Richard Daley. There was little doubt that a Kennedy was going to leave that city without the nomination. In fact, RFK manager Pierre Salinger confirmed this in 1995 in his book, *P.S: A Memoir*.

"When the first solid good news came in regarding California, I went upstairs to the suite to tell Bobby and to suggest it was time to go down to the ballroom. No, he said, he would wait a bit longer. We were sitting there talking when the phone rang, and it was Chicago's Mayor, Richard Daley," wrote Salinger, former press secretary for JFK. The news Daley had to share was a bombshell. "He was calling to make it official – he would now publicly support Robert F. Kennedy as the Democratic candidate for President in 1968. Bobby and I exchanged a look that we both knew meant only one thing – he had the nomination."[269] Not only that, a May 1968 poll had Republican Richard Nixon and Kennedy locked in statistical dead heat, showing that people under 30 years old favored RFK 44% to 33% over Nixon.[270] That meant that a large voter turnout from millions of baby boomers, many of whom wanted to end the Vietnam War and were just starting to vote, would likely have given Kennedy the presidency in November.

This was a chance that the CIA was not going to take.

Making the Connection

The official version of events for the Robert Kennedy assassination is that after finishing his victory speech at the Ambassador Hotel Ballroom in downtown Los Angeles, RFK made his way behind the stage through a kitchen pantry crammed with humanity. It was here that lone gunman Sirhan Sirhan shot at the New York State senator, mortally wounding him, as witnesses pried the gun from his hand. Just like with the JFK and MLK assassinations, the fallacy of the lone gunman who worked absent of any conspiracy was pushed on the public by the media almost immediately.

There are two primary reasons why this is counterintuitive. First, the assassin's own behavior, and second, the overwhelming evidence of a second shooter. In February 2011, Sirhan's attorney, William Pepper made a dramatic announcement. He was seeking to either gain a new trial for Sirhan, or have him released on parole for two reasons. First, the assassin was hypno-programmed by the CIA to commit the assassination, plus the shot that killed RFK could never have come from him. After years of hypnosis and examination by psychiatrists, Pepper said there was, "no doubt he does not remember the critical events. He is not feigning it. It's not an act. He does not remember it. It was very clear to me that this guy did not kill Bob Kennedy."[271] Sirhan asserted to his lawyers that he was "brainwashed" to commit the murder so that he could be the patsy, and the true forces behind the assassination would never be known. His lack of memory of the event, his trance-like behavior on the day of the shooting, and his automatic writing exercises in his journal (where he would obsessively write "RFK must die") are some of the factors that indicate he was a member of the CIA's MKULTRA program that trained robotic-like assassins. Sirhan's other lawyer Lawrence Teeter said that Sirhan was forced against his will to take part in this program that used drugs, chemicals, and sensory deprivation to control the will of the assassin, removing that person's culpability in the committing of the crime. The CIA conducted these secret experimental programs in the 1950s and 1960s at the height of the Cold War.[272] Not surprisingly, Sirhan's chance for a new trial, and for parole were both denied.[273]

The evidence for a second gunman is equally compelling, further proving the conspiracy. There are several factors that point to the existence of a second gun being fired at RFK. Hotel maitre d' Karl Uecker was leading Senator Kennedy through the kitchen pantry, so he had an up close view of the shooting. The autopsy for Robert Kennedy revealed that he was shot point blank in the back of the head.[274] Uecker insisted that Sirhan never got close enough to deliver that kind of kill shot.

I have told the police and testified during the trial (he meant the grand jury proceeding) that there was a distance of at least one and one-half feet between the muzzle of Sirhan's gun and Senator Kennedy's head. The revolver was directly in front of my nose. After Sirhan's second shot, I pushed his hand that held the revolver down, and pushed him onto the steam table. There is no way that the shots described in the autopsy could have come from Sirhan's gun. When I told this to the authorities, they told me that I was wrong. But I repeat now what I told them then: Sirhan never got close enough for a point-blank shot, never.[275]

The obvious point to make here is that if Sirhan could not possibly have shot Kennedy in the head, there was at least one other assassin in the room, waiting to murder RFK. This proves the existence of a conspiracy, and is supported by other evidence as well. Forensic analysis, backed up by the research of Sirhan's lawyers indicate that at least 13 shots were fired at Kennedy and other victims at the crime scene, but the alleged assassin's gun only had 8 shots in it.[276]

In addition, there are the statements of Kennedy fundraiser Nina Rhodes-Hughes, who was standing just a few feet away from the senator when the fatal shots rang out. She insisted that she saw a second gunman firing at Kennedy, but her statements to the authorities were altered against her will. "What has to come out is that there was another shooter to my right," Rhodes-Hughes said in April 2012. "The truth has got to be told. No more cover-ups." She also claimed that the FBI changed her statement to make it look like she told them that there were only 8 shots. "I never said eight shots. I never, never said it," she said. "There were more than eight shots ... There were at least 12, maybe 14. And I know there were because I heard the rhythm in my head."[277]

Morales Strikes Again

Having established the role of the CIA in this assassination and the existence of a conspiracy, let us make the further connection to the drug trade. There is strong evidence that CIA agent David Morales was at the crime scene for the assassination of Robert Kennedy. Morales may have served as a spotter, a shooter, or played some kind of support role, such as reconnaissance of the crime scene. It is useful to recall that E. Howard Hunt named him as one of the conspirators in the JFK assassination.

In November 2006, after a three year investigation, BBC filmmaker Shane O'Sullivan aired a documentary on the program *Newsnight* that identified CIA agent David Morales as being at the Ambassador Hotel on the night of the assassination. O'Sullivan also identified fellow CIA agents Gordon Campbell, and George Joannides as being present as well. O'Sullivan said that there was no reason these agents should have been in Los Angeles because they were mostly based out of Southeast Asia. The report included a quote from Morales who told his friends "I was in Dallas when we got the son of a bitch, and I was in Los Angeles when we got the little bastard."[278] This gives us the link to the drug trade. If you recall, Ted Shackley ordered Morales to help organize the drug trade and later Operation Phoenix which was designed to protect the drug trafficking, and perpetuate the Vietnam War.

There apparently was nothing this agency would fail to do to protect its interests in Southeast Asia. Morales was a merciless, ruthless operative with a smug unapologetic mindset who was perfect for carrying out the orders of his superior officers in the agency. However, there was one more reason why RFK was assassinated by the CIA, a potentially explosion aspect to this story that they could not let happen.

RFK's Obsession

The threat of ending the Vietnam War and the drug trade were certainly the CIA's primary motivating factors in the assassination of Robert Kennedy, but there was an even greater threat to their interests that was lurking out there in the shadows. Kennedy had been making his own inquiries into the assassination of his brother from the moment of the murder. On November 22, 1963, Kennedy angrily confronted CIA Director John McCone, asking him directly if his agency planned the assassination.[279]

RFK had a good legal mind, a tenacious personality, and was an excellent researcher. He had come to the conclusion over the course of years of investigation that the CIA had killed his brother. He later met with conspiracy researchers Penn Jones, Jr., and Walter Sheridan to seek out information on the assassination. He even visited the CIA station in Mexico City where Oswald visited before the shooting. RFK felt that the only way for the truth to come out would be for him to use the powers of the presidency to reopen the investigation, and bring justice to those who killed JFK.[280]

So along with his public proclamations to end the war, he was privately running for president to avenge his brother's death. If he became president, and the truth came out that the CIA had murdered JFK, (and perhaps the truth behind the Malcolm X and Martin Luther King killings as well) it could lead to several executions for treason, the end of the CIA, and a complete remaking of our government's intelligence apparatus.

Therefore, in the entire history of the Central Intelligence Agency there was probably not a more potent threat to their very existence than Robert Francis Kennedy. First, if he was elected president he would end the Vietnam War, which would kill off the drug trade. Second, if president he would prove that the CIA had killed his brother which would likely lead to a huge public outcry for retribution of the beloved slain leader, JFK. These things simply could not be allowed to transpire.

The tragedy then of the assassination of Robert Kennedy is not just the millions of people who would die in Southeast Asia after 1969, (when RFK could have assumed the presidency), but also the execution of truth and justice.

Chapter Five

Unfinished Lives

The impact of the loss of these men has been felt to this very day. Although difficult to quantify, there are three fundamental areas of impact that we will explore. First, the cost of the Vietnam War in terms of the lives lost and the economic resources wasted. Second, the impact on the lives of the poor, and third, the personal costs felt within the families of these four men.

The Costs of War

58,156 men died fighting the Vietnam War. 303,704 soldiers were wounded in action, while 23,214 of these were classified as being 100 percent disabled, and 5,283 lost at least one limb.[281] 76 percent came from working or middle class families.[282] 17,539 were married men.[283] The National Archives and Records Administration lists 728 combat deaths in Laos, 523 in Cambodia, and 178 in Thailand.[284] CNN claims that there were 1.3 million total deaths for all countries involved in the war combined.[285] Other sources put that number as being much higher. In 1991, former JFK Defense Secretary Robert McNamara conducted his own survey of communist casualties in the Vietnam War, and determined that 1.2 million Vietnamese civilians were killed, plus 1.158 million military deaths.[286] This does not include an estimated 200,000 Cambodian deaths, and another 100,000 in Laos.[287]

More than any other country in the world, Laos also continues to suffer from unexploded landmines. They were deployed decades ago by both sides in the Laotian civil war, some of which were bought by U.S. taxpayer dollars, and money obtained from the opium trade. "No country bears the scars of these weapons more than Laos in Southeast Asia. During the Vietnam War (in which Laos was officially neutral), U.S. planes dropped 260 million cluster bomb sub-munitions on the country, of which around 80 million did not explode," reported *The Guardian* in 2012. "A national study estimated that 50,000 people have been killed or injured by unexploded ordnance since 1964, and that there have been 20,000 casualties since the end of the war. Nearly 50 years later, Laos still averages four new victims every week."[288]

In addition to these numbers, it is difficult to determine exactly how many veterans have killed themselves as a result to exposure to the horrors of the Vietnam War. Thousands of veterans still suffer from post traumatic stress disorder and are likely to add to the total as time moves forward. In Chuck Dean's groundbreaking book *Nam Vet*, he asserts that 150,000 Vietnam veterans have taken their own lives since the war ended in 1975. He also found that the rate of divorce for Vietnam veterans is over 90 percent, and 500,000 vets have been arrested, or served jail time.[289]

In doing research for his book *Suicide Wall*, author Alexander Paul interviewed a VA doctor who said "the number of Vietnam veteran suicides was 200,000 men, and that the reason the official suicide statistics were so much lower was that in many cases the suicides were documented as accidents, primarily single-car drunk driving accidents and self inflicted gunshot wounds that were not accompanied by a suicide note...The under reporting of suicides was primarily an act of kindness to the surviving relatives."[290]

Adding to the misery is the wave of drug addiction prevalent among these war veterans. Heroin addiction led to many of these suicides, first offered to these men courtesy of the CIA. In 1973, Dr. Lee Robins did a study of Vietnam War soldiers and discovered that almost half of them had used heroin or opium at least once during their tour of duty. The study said that when returning from the war, "rather than giving up drugs altogether, many had shifted from heroin to amphetamines or barbiturates.

Nevertheless, almost none expressed a desire for treatment. Pre-service use of drugs and extent of use in Vietnam were the strongest predictors of continued use after Vietnam."[291] Of the 3.4 million men who served in active duty from 1964 to 1975, [292] it is estimated that after the war ended, as much as 75% of them at one point suffered from continued drug and alcohol abuse.[293]

The economic cost of the war was also astounding. On June 29, 2010, the Congressional Research Service prepared a report for all members of the U.S. Congress that was titled "Costs of Major U.S. Wars." The report states that "All estimates are of the costs of military operations only and do not include costs of veterans benefits, interest paid for borrowing money to finance wars, or assistance to allies." The non-disclosed "black budgets" of the CIA are also not included in the estimate either, nor money spent in the decade of occupation prior to 1965, or the economic costs of taking care of a generation of damaged veterans. The report concluded (when adjusted for inflation for projected year 2011) that between 1965 and 1975 the United States spent a staggering $738 billion losing the Vietnam War.[294] This figure easily tops $1 trillion if that which was excluded is put into the estimate. Such an amount could have won Lyndon Johnson's war on poverty. About 12%[295] of the U.S. population of 216 million people[296] were living in poverty in 1975 when the war ended. That is nearly 26 million people. The $1 trillion spent on the war could have provided each of these people with a check worth $36,461, giving a family of four living in poverty over $153,000. Imagine what a $1 trillion stimulus of savings and spending within the U.S. economy could have done for job growth, and the health of the middle class, which brings us to the second impact that the deaths of these four men caused.

The United States of Inequality

Much has been written about the current state of economic inequality in the United States. Little has been understood though about how history got us to this point. Whether you view this inequality as a positive or negative reality, the fact is that it exists to a degree rarely seen in U.S. history. The past several decades have witnessed a dramatic shift in wealth into the hands of a miniscule class of people. In the past thirty five years, (in other words about when RFK could have finished his second term), the share of U.S. income going to the top 1 percent has doubled, and that of the top 0.1 percent has nearly tripled.[297] In fact, by 2013 the top 1 percent has been able to capture 46 percent of the world's wealth.[298] The wealth of the top 400 American families is equal to that of half the population of the United States, approximately 150 million people.[299]

"Greater income and wealth in the hands of top income earners gives them greater access to legislators. And it confers more ability to influence public opinion through contributions to research organizations and political action committees," said Cornell University economist Robert Frank. "The results have included long term reductions in income and estate taxes, as well as relaxed business regulations. These changes in turn have caused further concentrations of income and wealth at the top, creating even more political influence."[300]

In examining the reasons for this historical shift, rarely has any commentator linked the tragedies of the 1960s with our current state of affairs. This is a mistake. A world where these men lived out their lives, probably into the late 1990s, would have produced a much different world today. These four leaders were some of the most effective, charismatic, and vocal defenders of the working class that this country has yet to see. With their voices silent, it has been become much easier to ignore these needs without their effective leadership.

Martin Luther King's Poor People's Campaign would surely have achieved unmeasured levels of success during a Robert Kennedy administration. RFK had made a point of drawing attention to poverty in Mississippi as a U.S. senator. We noted earlier as well that when he announced for the presidency he specifically said that he was running for president in part to end the gap between the rich and the poor. He certainly would have been a key ally in the White House into the 1970s, as MLK moved into the next phase of his life while still a young man in his early 40s. With the Vietnam War over during an RFK administration there would be no invasions of Laos or Cambodia, and thus no shootings at Kent State or Jackson State University in 1970. Watergate would still be an apartment/office complex in Washington, and not a synonym for scandal and corruption.

With 8 to 16 years of the Kennedys in the White House, there would have been a shift to the needs of the working class, pushed by the growing movements of Malcolm X and MLK, who would continue to hold the administrations accountable to the interests of the vast majority of Americans. Access to the government would not be given to the wealthy, but instead to a broader class of people. The middle class would flourish with a trillion dollars that would never have been wasted in Vietnam, instead invested in the United States. Public works programs along the lines of the New Deal to employ the working class and repair the damaged environment would bring spending power to millions of people.

Malcolm X would have continued to strengthen U.S. – African relations in the late 1960s with visits by President Robert Kennedy to bring a new era of cooperation with the African continent to heal the wounds inflicted by CIA assassinations. In fact, with the revelations of truth behind the JFK assassination, and the dismantling of the CIA by President Robert Kennedy, the U.S. would see fewer backlashes to its foreign policy. Anti-American sentiment would erode with the absence of this agency, and the continued work by Malcolm X to promote U.S. – African unity. It is difficult to envision Africa being a seed bed for anti-American terrorism with the CIA gone, and Malcolm X working for decades with African leaders. RFK would likely make him an ambassador to any nation of his choosing to heal this relationship, much like the Good Neighbor Policy of FDR that repaired friendships with Latin America after decades of military meddling in Central and South America.

These four men were advocates for the working class, for the common man. They were all men of peace, even Malcolm X who never advocated violence for the sake of violence, spoke out against the Vietnam War, and sought cooperation with Dr. King. With these four men alive for decades to come it is difficult to imagine a lack of faith, a lack of respect, and a lack of confidence in the very idea of government. It is impossible to envision these four men allowing the wealthy to kidnap the wealth and power of this nation from a whole class of people. They were all from a generation that grew up with the idea that America could do great things, and justice was a goal to be fought for. I doubt they would stand by if the class of people they championed in their lives needed their help to correct this injustice. Furthermore, it is difficult to envision this inequality even existing in the first place if they were afforded that most basic of human rights: to live.

Fathers and Husbands

Americans sometimes think of these four slain leaders in mythological terms, perhaps because of how they died. Nevertheless, we should pause to consider that all of them were fathers and husbands. It is not our place to judge whether they were good family men, but the fact remains that these assassinations left four women without their husbands, and many children without their fathers, all at a young age.

John F. Kennedy and his wife Jacqueline had two surviving children. Caroline was just about to turn six years-old at the time of the assassination,[301] while John, Jr., turned three years-old on the day of his father's funeral, November 25, 1963.[302]

Malcolm X and his wife Betty were the parents of six children, all girls: Qubilah, Malikah, Attallah, Ilaysah, Gamilah, and Malaak.[303] Many of them went on to live troubled lives. Qubilah, who witnessed her own father's death, was four years-old at the time of the shooting. She later took a plea deal to avoid prison in an alleged plot to kill Louis Farrakhan, whom she believed conspired to kill her father. As part of the agreement she underwent treatment for drug and alcohol abuse.[304] At the time of the assassination, Betty was pregnant with twin girls. When they were born on September 30, 1965, she named them Malikah, and Malaak, both in honor of her late husband. In 2011, Malikah was sentenced to probation in connection with charges of identity theft, forgery, and cheating a woman out of thousands of dollars.[305] Attallah was six years-old at the time of her father's death, and is probably the most renowned of all the children, working now as an artist, human rights activist, lecturer, actress, and theatrical producer.[306] Ilaysah was two years-old when she witnessed her father's assassination, and has gone on to write a successful book about her family called *Growing Up X* (Random House, 2002).[307] Gamilah was less than a year old, and in her mother's arms while Betty watched her husband get shot to death in February 1965. She was given the middle name Lumumba, named after Patrice Lumumba of the Congo, a hero of Malcolm X whom the CIA also killed.[308]

Martin Luther King and his wife Coretta had four children: two sons, and two daughters. Yolanda was 12 years-old when her father was murdered. She grew up around much of the turmoil of the Civil Rights Movement, later going on to become a human rights activist, playwright, and lecturer. She died on May 15, 2007.[309] Martin Luther King III was ten years-old when his father was assassinated, later going on to become a human rights activist and community organizer, like his sister. In 1998, he was elected to lead his father's Southern Christian Leadership Conference.[310] Dexter was seven years-old at the time of his father's death, and also later went onto to head the SCLC.[311] Bernice was the youngest sibling. She had just turned five years-old a week before her father's death, and later followed in her father's footsteps by becoming a minister.[312]

Robert Kennedy and his wife Ethel had eleven children: Kathleen, Joseph, Robert, David, Mary Courtney, Michael, Mary Kerry, Matthew, Christopher, Douglas, and Rory. Their births spanned from 1951 to 1968. The oldest children were teenagers when their father was assassinated, while Ethel was pregnant with Rory at the time of the shooting.[313]

The CIA left 23 children without a father.

Jacqueline Kennedy's Final Lament

One of the strengths of John F. Kennedy as a president was his ability to evolve as a world leader, to move from the Cold War rhetoric that helped elect him president to becoming a man dedicated to peace. From his Peace Corps to Cuba, Vietnam, and Laos, he proved to be a man who could see the need to change things.

At the end of his short time on this earth it privately appeared that he was doing this with his personal life as well. His extramarital affairs are well documented and there is no need to rehash them here. What has only recently come to light though is that in the last few months of his life, JFK was becoming increasingly closer to Jacqueline and making key steps to repair his damaged marriage with her, including ending the relationships with his various girlfriends. The turning point for them as couple was the death of their son Patrick. This little boy arrived over five weeks early, and weighed just over four pounds and 10 ounces. After a two day struggle for life, Patrick Bouvier Kennedy died on August 9, 1963, at the Children's Medical Center in Boston.[314] The president slept in the hospital overnight and held his infant son in his arms just before he died. Afterwards, he placed a phone call to his brother Edward Kennedy, and the hospital staff could clearly hear him sobbing through the door.

When Mrs. Kennedy emerged from Otis Air Force Base Hospital, one week after the birth, she and the president walked hand in hand to the presidential limousine. "After the death of Patrick, the other agents and I noticed a distinctly closer relationship, openly expressed, between the president and Mrs. Kennedy," said Secret Service agent Clint Hill, one of the many agents who would fail the president in Dallas. "I first observed it in the hospital suite at Otis Air Force Base but it became publicly visible when Mrs. Kennedy was released from the hospital."[315] The fact that the president and first lady emerged holding hands was significant. "It was a small gesture, but quite significant to those of us who were around them all the time. Prior to this, they were much more restrained and less willing to express their close, loving relationship while out in public. The loss of Patrick seemed to be the catalyst to change all that."[316]

Press Secretary Pierre Salinger also noticed the new relationship. "The death of the infant was one of the hardest moments in the lives of both the President and Mrs. Kennedy," he said. "The White House had brought about a closeness in their relationship, a wider understanding of one another. The death of their baby brought them even closer."[317]

Jackie Kennedy rarely made campaign appearances with her husband, so her decision to accompany him to Dallas was significant. Historian William Manchester for years covered up the fact that on Air Force One, just hours before the shooting, the presidential couple took some private time to be sexually intimate.[318] JFK even made a point to compliment his wife during his final speech, saying that once again he felt like the man accompanying Mrs. Kennedy, like during their trip to Paris.[319]

It was clear that there was a rebirth in their marriage; that Mrs. Kennedy had finally got her husband back, and then tragedy struck in a cruel twist of fate. The devastation she felt was clearly demonstrated in a letter she wrote to her minister, Washington Auxiliary Bishop Philip Hannan, who delivered JFK's eulogy. Mrs. Kennedy wrote to him to thank the priest for his support in a time of need.

"I haven't believed in the child's vision of heaven for a long time. There is no way now to commune with him. It will be so long before I am dead and even then I don't know if I will be reunited with him," she wrote on December 20, 1963. "Even if I am I don't think you could ever convince me that it will be the way it was while we were married here. Please forgive all this – and please don't try to convince me just yet – I shouldn't be writing this way."[320]

In this haunting peak into her soul, Mrs. Kennedy summed up the feelings of the entire nation in one sentence. In fact, these words apply not just to when JFK died, but when his brother was killed, along with Malcolm X, and Dr. King.

"If only I could believe that he could look down and see how he is missed, and how nobody will ever be the same without him."[321]

References

1. http://www.catholicculture.org/culture/library/view.cfm ?id =7389&CFID=29248120&CFTOKEN= 33556540

2. Gary Donaldson, The First Modern Campaign: Kennedy, Nixon, and the Election of 1960 (Lanham, Maryland: Rowman and Littlefield Publishers, 2007), 107.

3. "Auction of JFK items includes doodle found in Houston trash can," http://blog.chron.com/thetexican/2013/11/auction-of-jfk-items-includes-doodle-found-in-houston-trash-can/#17745101=0.
    Kennedy sketched a doodle of a sailboat on some stationery inside his room at the Rice Hotel, which was subsequently auctioned in 2013. The date of this speech was September 12, 1960, JFK's seven year wedding anniversary.

4. http://www.americanrhetoric.com/speeches/jfkhouston-ministers.html

5. Ibid.

6. Ibid.

7. http://presidentelect.org/e1960.html

8. "What Dallas Pastors Preached the Sunday after JFK was killed," http://www.religionnews.com/2013/11/19/jfk-sermons-process/

9. Ibid.

10. President Kennedy Has Been Shot (Naperville, Illinois: Sourcebooks, Inc., 2003), audio cd, track 16, "Citizens and Broadcasters React."

11. http://www.nola.com/opinions/index.ssf/2013/11/hatred_of_catholics_led_some_t.html

12. http://www.independent.co.uk/life-style/were-heading-into-nut-country-president-kennedy-said-this-to-an-aide-

as-he-began-his-fatal-visit-to-texas-thirty-years-ago-here-peter-pringle-evokes-dallas-as-it-was-then-a-hostile-place-which-cared-very-little-for-the-dream-that-died-there-1505387.html

13. Ibid.
14. http://www.dallasnews.com/news/jfk50/explore/20130307-dallas-dealey-plaza-restoration-nears-completion.ece
15. http://www.independent.co.uk/life-style/were-heading-into-nut-country-president-kennedy-said-this-to-an-aide-as-he-began-his-fatal-visit-to-texas-thirty-years-ago-here-peter-pringle-evokes-dallas-as-it-was-then-a-hostile-place-which-cared-very-little-for-the-dream-that-died-there-1505387.html
16. Ibid.
17. http://www.pbs.org/wgbh/americanexperience/features/general-article/kennedys-and-civil-rights/
18. http://library.thinkquest.org/J0112391/jfk.htm
19. http://www.history.com/this-day-in-history/kennedy-announces-fair-housing-legislation
20. http://www.pbs.org/wnet/african-americans-many-rivers-to-cross/history/how-black-was-jfks-camelot/
21. http://www.spartacus.schoolnet.co.uk/JFKbolden.htm
22. http://microsites.jfklibrary.org/olemiss/home/
23. http://library.thinkquest.org/J0112391/jfk.htm
24. http://www.pbs.org/wgbh/americanexperience/features/primary-resources/jfk-civilrights/
25. http://www.independent.co.uk/life-style/...
26. Karl Evanzz The Judas Factor: The Plot to Kill Malcolm X (New York: Thunder's Mouth Press, 1992), 98.
27. The JFK library website has extensive information on the invasion that can be found here: http://www.jfklibrary.org/JFK/JFK-in-History/The-Bay-of-Pigs.aspx
28. http://www.nytimes.com/1994/02/08/obituaries/richard-m-

bissell-84-is-dead-helped-plan-bay-of-pigs-invasion.html

29. "Gen. Charles Cabell Dies, Former CIA Deputy Director" The Washington Post 27 May 1971. New Orleans District Attorney Jim Garrison suspected Cabell was also one of the co-conspirators in the assassination of JFK. See "Garrison Planned To Link General To JFK Slaying" The Washington Post 16 September 1973for more on this.

30. "CIA: Marker of Policy or Tool? survey finds widely feared agency is tightly controlled" *New York Times*. April 25, 1966.

31. http://www.ratical.org/ratville/JFK/USO/appE.html. NSAM 56 incidentally was simply an inventory. review of paramilitary operations ordered by National Security Advisor McGeorge Bundy.

32. Ibid.

33. http://www.history.com/this-day-in-history/united-states-and-soviet-union-will-establish-a-hot-line

34. http://www.spacedaily.com/news/russia-97h.html

35. http://www.jfklibrary.org/JFK/JFK-in-History/Nuclear-Test-Ban-Treaty.aspx?p=2

36. http://jfkfacts.org/assassination/experts/was-jfk-going-to-pull-out-of-vietnam/

37. http://www.news.yahoo.com/13-documents-read-jfk-assassination

38. http://www.peacecorps.gov/about/history/

39. http://www.bibliotecapleyades.net/sociopolitica/esp_sociopol_secretgov_5i.htm

40. http://www.jfklibrary.org/Asset-Viewer/Archives/JFKPOF-TPH-17B-1.aspx. The full recording can be heard here.

41. http://ratical.org/ratville/JFK/Unspeakable/Item03.pdf

42. http://www.bibliotecapleyades.net/sociopolitica/esp_sociopol_secretgov_5i.htm

43. http://www.peacecorps.gov/about/jobs/workingpc/eligibility/

44. http://www.maryferrell.org/wiki/index.php/Operation_

Northwoods.
For more information on Operation Northwoods see James Bamford's book Body of Secrets (Anchor Books, 2002).

45. http://jfkfacts.org/assassination/on-this-date/dec-22-1963-truman-calls-for-abolition-of-cia/

46. http://www.pewresearch.org/fact-tank/2013/11/20/jfks-america/

47. Charles Crenshaw, JFK: Conspiracy of Silence (New York: Penguin Books, 1992), 79.

48. "Doctor's Report: Two Wounds, Throat and Head" *San Francisco Chronicle* 23 November 1963.

49. http://www.biography.com/people/e-howard-hunt-262375?page=1.

50. Vincent Bugliosi, Reclaiming History: The Assassination of President John F. Kennedy (New York: W. W. Norton & Company, 2007), 930.

51. Ibid.

52. http://www.apfn.org/apfn/mockingbird.htm

53. "The Last Confession of E. Howard Hunt" *Rolling Stone* 5 April 2007.

54. http://jfkfacts.org/assassination/top-6-jfk-files-the-cia-still-keeps-secret/

55. http://jfkfacts.org/assassination/news/key-jfk-files-ignored-in-obama-declassification-drive/

56. http://www.merriam-webster.com/dictionary/treason

57. Spencer Tucker and Priscilla Mary Roberts, eds., World War One: A Student Encyclopedia (New York: ABC-CLIO, 2005), 1205.

58. http://www.history.com/this-day-in-history/eisenhower-gives-famous-domino-theory-speech

59. http://www.amazon.com/Kill-Messenger-Crack-Cocaine-Controversy-Journalist/dp/1560259302/ref=pd_cp_b_2.
More can read about his tragic story in the book Kill the Messenger by Nick Schou, available through this link.

60. http://www.nytimes.com/2007/09/16/weekinreview/16 fuller.html?_r=0

61. http://www.u-s-history.com/pages/h1875.html

62. Nixon, Richard, RN: The Memoirs of Richard Nixon (New York: Grosset & Dunlap, 1978)

63. "CIA: Maker of Policy or Tool?" New York Times 26 April 1966. This article was one of many things to inspire New Orleans District Attorney Jim Garrison to pursue an investigation against the CIA. The article also notes how the president, unlike Eisenhower, allowed American ambassadors to have more authority abroad than CIA agents such as in Yemen.

64. Jacob Van Staaveren, Interdiction in Southern Laos, 1960-1968 (Washington, D.C.: U.S. Government Printing Office, 1993), 1.

65. Ibid., 2.

66. Ibid., 3.

67. Edmund F. Wehrle, "'A Good, Bad Deal:' John F. Kennedy, W. Averell Harriman, and the Neutralization of Laos, 1961-1962," Pacific Historical Review 67, no. 3 (August 1998): 352.

68. Robert S. McNamara, Argument Without End: In Search of Answers to the Vietnam Tragedy (New York: Public Affairs, 1999), 104.

69. Ibid.

70. Ibid.

71. Geoffery Warner, "President Kennedy and Indochina: The 1961 Decisions," International Affairs 70, no. 4 (1994): 686.

72. McNamara, 104.

73. Ibid.

74. Richard Reeves, President Kennedy: Profile of Power (New York: Simon and Schuster, 1993), 30. The account of this meeting is based on notes taken by Clark Clifford, Kennedy's personal lawyer and transition chief, who attended the meeting.

75. Ibid., 31.

76. Ibid.

77. Ibid.

78. Ibid.

79. William J. Duiker, U.S. Containment Policy and the Conflict in Indochina (Stanford, California: Stanford University Press, 1994), 255.

80. Van Staaveren, 7.

81. Ibid.

82. Ibid., 9.

83. Ibid.

84. Federal Research Division, Laos: A Country Study, 3rd ed. (Washington, D.C.: Government Printing Office, 1995), xxv.

85. Warner, 688.

86. Reeves, 309.

87. Ibid.

88. Reeves, 111.

89. Ibid.

90. Wehrle, 353.

91. Ibid., 357.

92. Ibid.

93. Jane Hamilton-Merritt, Tragic Mountains: The Hmong, the Americans, and the Secret Wars for Laos, 1942-1992 (Indianapolis, Indiana: Indiana University Press, 1993), 113.

94. Ibid., 114.

95. Van Staaveren, 7.

96. Ibid., 8.

97. Reeves, 46.

98. Ibid., 47.

99. Ibid.

100. William J. Lederer and Eugene Burdick, The Ugly American (New York: W. W. Norton and Company, 1958), 283.

101. Reeves, 69.

102. Ibid.
103. Federal Research Division, 58.
104. Ibid., 281.
105. Reeves, 221.
106. Ibid.
107. Hamilton-Merritt, 3.
108. Ibid.
109. Ibid., xviii.
110. Federal Research Division, 58.
111. Martin E. Goldstein, American Policy Toward Laos (Cranbury, New Jersey: Associated University Presses), 320.
112. Ibid., 321.
113. Ibid., 324.
114. Ibid.
115. Ibid., 320.
116. McNamara, 105.
117. Warner, 687.
118. Ibid., 688.
119. Duiker, 253.
120. Ibid., 257.
121. Ibid.
122. Goldstein, 234.
123. Duiker, 257.
124. Wehrle, 354.
125. Reeves, 75.
126. Goldstein, 235.
127. Van Staaveren, 15.
128. Wehrle, 355.
129. Richard Nixon, RN: The Memoirs of Richard Nixon (New York: Grosset & Dunlap, 1978), 235.
130. Warner, 690.
131. Ibid., 692.
132. Reeves, 116.
133. Goldstein, 250.

134. Wehrle, 360.

135. Noam Kochavi, "Limited Accommodation, Perpetuated Conflict: Kennedy, China, and the Laos Crisis, 1961-1963," Diplomatic History 26, no. 1 (Winter 2002): 98.

136. Ibid., 101.

137. Ibid., 100.

138. Wehrle, 363.

139. Ibid.

140. Reeves, 238.

141. Van Staaveren, 10.

142. Ibid.

143. Ibid.

144. Ibid., 11. Van Staaveren provides no exact date for this report.

145. Wehrle, 362.

146. Ibid., 365.

147. Ibid.

148. Tape No. 11A/XX2A, "Laos," (Boston, Massachusetts: John Fitzgerald Kennedy Library, 21 August 1962.)

149. Goldstein, 255.

150. Ibid.

151. Ibid.

152. Alfred W. McCoy, The Politics of Heroin: CIA Complicity in the Global Drug Trade (Chicago: Lawrence Hill Books, 1972), 161.

153. Ibid, 162.

154. "U.S. Blames Rightists," New York Times 7 May 1962.

155. Ibid.

156. Reeves, 307.

157. Ibid.

158. "Rebels Capture Laotian Center," New York Times 7 May 1962.

159. "C.I.A. is Blamed for Laos Crisis," Times (London) 16 May 1962.

160. Ibid.

161. Duiker, 286.
162. Reeves, 310.
163. Ibid.
164. Van Staaveren, 5.
165. Goldstein, 264.
166. Ibid.
167. World Book Encyclopedia, 1998 ed., s.v. "Laos."
168. Goldstein, 267.
169. Ibid.
170. McNamara, 110.
171. Kochavi, 119.
172. Ibid., 121. The administration felt that this border war was opportunistic and aggressive since it took place during the Cuban Missile Crisis.
173. McNamara, 109.
174. Ibid.
175. Wehrle, 372.
176. Ibid.
177. Hamilton-Merritt, 120.
178. Ibid.
179. Van Staaveren, 5.
180. http://millercenter.org/president/speeches/detail/5762
181. Ibid.
182. Hamilton-Merritt, 120.
183. Tape No. 11A/XX2A, "Laos," (Boston, Massachusetts: John Fitzgerald Kennedy Library, 21 August 1962.
184. Goldstein, 292.
185. Ibid., 293.
186. Ibid., 121.
187. Reeves, 483.
188. Ibid.
189. Wilfred Burchett, The Furtive War: The United States in Laos and Vietnam (New York: International Publishers, 1963), postscript.

190. Ibid.
191. Ibid.
192. Van Staaveren, 19.
193. http://archiver.rootsweb.ancestry.com/th/read/HERRICK /2003-06/1056847458
194. The above analysis of the crash story is taken from an excellent tribute for Merrick written by Associated Press reporter Robert Burns that can be found at this link: http://www.air-america.org/newspaper_articles/herrick. shtml
195. Ibid.
196. McCoy, 95.
197. http://www.amazon.com/The-Politics-Heroin-Complicity-Global/dp/1556524838/ref=sr_1_sc_1?ie=UTF8&qid=13892 25672&sr=8-1-spell&keywords=cia+drugtrafficking
198. http://www.lbjlib.utexas.edu/johnson/archives.hom/nsams /nsam273.asp
199. http://consortiumnews.com/2013/05/08/the-almost-scoop-on-nixons-treason-2/
200. http://www.spartacus.schoolnet.co.uk/JFKshackley.htm
201. Ibid.
202. Ibid.
203. Ibid.
204. McCoy, 163
205. This brief summary of Malcolm X's life is drawn from: Miriam Sagan, Mysterious Deaths: Malcolm X (San Diego: Lucent Books, 1997)
206. Karl Evanzz, The Judas Factor: The Plot to Kill Malcolm X (New York: Thunder's Mouth Press, 1992), 76 and 318.
207. Ibid., 294.
208. James W. Douglass, "The Murder and Martyrdom of Malcolm," The Assassinations: Probe Magazine on JFK, MLK, RFK, and Malcolm X (Los Angeles: Feral House, 2003), 409.

209. Evanzz, 255.
210. Ibid., 256.
211. Ibid.
212. Sagan, 25.
213. Ibid., 68.
214. Douglass, 404.
215. Ibid.
216. Ibid. 411.
217. http://www.aavw.org/protest/homepage_malcolmx.html
218. http://www.edchange.org/multicultural/speeches/malcolm_x_ballot.html
219. http://www.aavw.org/protest/homepage_malcolmx.html
220. http://www.aavw.org/protest/homepage_malcolmx.html
221. http://pascf.org.uk/resources/liw5+-+Malcolm+X+on+drugs.pdf
222. Ibid.
223. See a clip of this speech at:
     http://www.youtube.com/watch?v=P2n-1902lyg
224. http://www.blackpast.org/1964-malcolm-x-s-speech-founding-rally-organization-afro-american-unity
225. Read the full speech at:
     http://www.blackpast.org/1964-malcolm-x-s-speech-founding-rally-organization-afro-american-unity
226. http://www.maryferrell.org/wiki/index.php/Warren_Commission
227. http://www.pbs.org/wgbh/americanexperience/freedom-riders/people/james-farmer
228. Sagan, 73.
229. Ibid.
230. Evanzz, xx.
231. Danny Schechter, The More You Watch the Less You Know: News Wars/(sub)Merged Hopes/Media Adventures (New York: Seven Stories Press, 1997), 288.
232. Ibid.

233. Ibid., 287
234. Ibid.
235. Ezanzz, 97
236. http://www.core-online.org/History/james_farmer.htm
237. Ibid.
238. Ezanzz, 37.
239. Ibid., 277.
240. http://www.pbs.org/wgbh/americanexperience/freedom-riders/people/james-farmer.
The case of James Farmer reminds me certain figures in the assassination of Martin Luther King, Jr., who avoided death and prosecution because of secret services rendered to their country. William Pepper discusses this in his book on the King assassination titled "An Act of State: The Execution of Martin Luther King." Perhaps it is not surprising then that this rather marginal civil rights figure was given the highest award for a civilian, the Presidential Medal of Freedom, in 1998.
241. Evanzz, 227.
242. Ibid., 229.
243. Ibid., 230.
244. Ibid., 231.
245. Ibid., 244.
246. William Pepper, An Act of State: The Execution of Martin Luther King (New York: Verso, 2003), 177.
247. James W. Douglass, "The King Conspiracy Exposed in Memphis ," The Assassinations: Probe Magazine on JFK, MLK, RFK, and Malcolm X (Los Angeles: Feral House, 2003), 504.
248. http://www.spartacus.schoolnet.co.uk/JFKshackley.htm
249. Pepper, 96.
250. Ibid., 120.
251. Douglass, 503
252. Ibid., 502.

253. http://www.amistadresource.org/civil_rights_era/black_opposition_to_vietnam.html
254. http://www.americanrhetoric.com/speeches/mlkatimeto-breaksilence.htm
255. Ibid.
256. Ibid.
257. Ibid.
258. http://www.informationclearinghouse.info/article16183.htm
259. http://www.examiner.com/article/mlk-quotes-you-are-unlikely-to-hear-on-fox-news-or-glenn-beck-s-show-today
260. http://mlk-kpp01.stanford.edu/index.php/resources/article/king_quotes_on_war_and_peace/
261. http://www.historyandtheheadlines.abc-clio.com/ContentPages/ContentPage.aspx?entryId=1194576&currentSection=1194544
262. http://www.4president.org/Speeches/1968/rfk1968announcement.htm
263. Ibid.
264. Ibid.
265. Ibid.
266. http://www.pbs.org/wgbh/amex/rfk/filmmore/ps_ksu.html
267. http://museumca.org/theoaklandstandard/mr-kennedy-and-1968-battle-california
268. "Resnick Concedes in Early Morning Defeat" *New York Times* 19 June 1968
269. Pierre Salinger, P.S: A Memoir (New York: St. Martin's Press, 1995), 196.
270. http://www.pewresearch.org/fact-tank/2013/06/05/polling-flashback-remembering-rfk/
271. http://www.dailymail.co.uk/news/article-1361455/Robert-Kennedy-assassin-Sirhan-Bishara-claims-I-brainwashed-freedom-bid.html
272. http://www.examiner.com/article/rfk-assassination-sirhan-

sirhan-and-brainwashing-conspiracies
273. http://www.cbsnews.com/news/rfk-assassin-sirhan-sirhan-denied-parole/
274. William Klaber and Philip H. Melanson, Shadow Play: The Murder of Robert F. Kennedy, The Trial of Sirhan Sirhan and the Failure of American Justice (New York: St. Martin's Press, 1997), 97.
275. Ibid., 95-96.
276. http://www.dailymail.co.uk/news/article-1361455/Robert-Kennedy-assassin-Sirhan-Bishara-claims-I-brainwashed-freedom-bid.html
277. http://www.huffingtonpost.com/2012/04/30/rfk-assassi-nation-nina-rhodes-hughes_n_1464439.html
278. http://news.bbc.co.uk/2/hi/programmes/newsnight/6169006.stm
279. "The Assassination: Was it a Conspiracy?" Time 2 July 2007
280. Ibid.
281. http://www.mrfa.org/vnstats.htm
282. http://www.veteranshour.com/vietnam_war_statistics.htm
283. Ibid.
284. http://www.archives.gov/research/military/vietnam-war/casualty-statistics.html
285. http://www.cnn.com/2013/07/01/world/vietnam-war-fast-facts/
286. http://faculty.washington.edu/charles/new%20PUBS/A77.pdf
287. http://alphahistory.com/vietnam/costs-of-the-vietnam-war/
288. http://www.theguardian.com/global-development/poverty-matters/2012/jul/06/landmines-toll-civilians-laos-bombs
289. http://winoverptsd.com/wp/category/disturbing-facts-about-vietnam-veterans/
290. http://www.suicidewall.com/suicide-statistics/
291. http://aje.oxfordjournals.org/content/99/4/235.short
292. http://www.veteranshour.com/vietnam_war_statistics.htm

293. http://winoverptsd.com/wp/some-disturbing-facts-about-vietnam-veterans/
294. https://www.fas.org/sgp/crs/natsec/RS22926.pdf
295. http://www.jstor.org/discover/10.2307/145499?uid=3739832&uid=2129&uid=2&uid=70&uid=4&uid=3739256&sid=21103441375783
296. http://www.multpl.com/united-states-population/table
297. "Arguments for 'Inequality'" *The Nation* 10 February 2014
298. http://www.huffingtonpost.com/2013/10/09/richest-1-percent-wealth_n_4072658.html
299. http://www.cnbc.com/id/101038089
300. "Arguments for 'Inequality'" *The Nation* 10 February 2014
301. http://www.biography.com/people/caroline-kennedy-204598
302. http://www.biography.com/people/john-f-kennedy-jr-9542094
303. https://www.google.com/#q=Malcolm%20X%20children
304. "Settlement Reached in Murder-for-Hire Case Against Malcolm X's Daughter, Qubilah Shabazz" *Jet* 15May 1995
305. "Malcolm X's daughter, Malikah Shabazz, gets five years probation for swindle of elderly widow" *Daily News* 28 July 2011
306. http://www.answers.com/topic/attallah-shabazz
307. http://www.ilyasahshabazz.com/page/ilyasah-shabazz.html
308. http://books.google.com/books?id=L8QMDYJAIJoC&pg=PA197&lpg=PA197&dq=gamilah+lumumba&source=bl&ots=txVg0X8uhT&sig=SfqO1ukKcdc2UBSi7tekgSmewD8&hl=en&sa=X&ei=KKjvUuSKBceEyAH33YDgCg&ved=0CE4Q6AEwCQ#v=onepage&q=gamilah%20lumumba&f=false
309. http://www.nytimes.com/2007/05/17/us/17king.html?_r=0
310. http://www.nytimes.com/2001/07/26/us/a-civil-rights-group-suspends-then-reinstates-its-president.html
311. Ibid. Dexter is a staunch defender of the conspiracy theories surrounding his father's death.

312. http://www.cnn.com/2013/08/25/us/bernice-king-profile/
313. https://www.google.com/#q=Robert+F.+Kennedy's+children
314. http://www.washingtonpost.com/opinions/for-john-and-jackie-kennedy-the-death-of-a-son-may-have-brought-them-closer/2013/10/24/2506051e-369b-11e3-ae46-e4248e75c8ea_story.html
315. Ibid.
316. Ibid.
317. Ibid.
318. http://www.dailymail.co.uk/news/article-2508767/JFK-Jackie-Kennedy-sex-Air-Force-One-day-death.html
319. President Kennedy Has Been Shot (Naperville, Illinois: Sourcebooks, Inc., 2003), audio cd, track 2.
320. http://www.thedailybeast.com/articles/2010/06/01/kennedy-funeral-and-jackie-onassis-letters-by-archbisop-hannan.html
321. Ibid.

Chronos Books is a historical non-fiction imprint. Chronos
publishes real history for real people; bringing to life historical
people, places and events in an imaginative, easy-to-digest and
accessible way. We want writers of historical books, from ancient
times to the Second World War, that will add to our
understanding of people and events rather than being
a dry textbook; history that passes on its stories to
a generation of new readers.